Other Books

The _ _ _
Growing To The Next Level

The Blessed Place
Living On Another Level

Conferences, Workshops, Seminars, & Courses Taught by Reginald D. Taylor

Discipleship & Leadership in the 21st Century
Concentrating Your Spiritual-Gifts & Influence Toward Making Disciples

Leadership for Life-Change
Biblical Lessons for Biblical Leaders

The Revolution
Developing the Spiritual Disciplines of Studying the Bible, Praying, & Fasting

The Blessed Place
A Study of the Book of Ephesians

Kingdom Living
A Study of the Book of Colossians

The Bible & The Believer
Learning & Applying the Principles of Bible Interpretation

The Life of The Preacher
Devotional Time-Developmental Time-Discovery Time, & Disciple-Making-Time

The Leadership of The Preacher
Being Studious, Stable, Steadfast, & Standardized

Old Testament & New Testament Surveys
Developing a Biblical & Systematic Theology Through a Working Knowledge of the Whole of Scripture

THE PREPARED LIFE
Kingdom Principles for Kingdom People

CONTENTS

Introduction

SECTION ONE
Principles from the Apostle's Praise

CHAPTER ONE: 9
THE PRIORITY THAT WAS REVEALED

CHAPTER TWO 16
THE PROCESS OF REPRODUCTION

CHAPTER THREE: 23
THE PRAISE THAT WAS RELEASED

SECTION TWO
Principles from the Apostle's Prayer

CHAPTER FOUR: 54
BE FILLED WITH THE WORD OF GOD
- ➤ Reading the Word
- ➤ Receiving the Word
- ➤ Researching the Word
- ➤ Reflecting on the Word
- ➤ Remembering the Word
- ➤ Reciting the Word
- ➤ Reverencing the Word
- ➤ Referencing the Word
- ➤ Responding to the Word

CHAPTER FIVE
BE FAITHFUL IN OUR WALK WITH GOD 70
- − The Requirement of Faithfulness
- − The Restraints of Faithfulness
- − The Refuge of Faithfulness
- − The Rewards of Faithfulness

CHAPTER SIX   84
BE FOCUSED ON THE WILL OF GOD
- ❖ Staying in the Literature of the Word
- ❖ Studying the Lessons of the Word
- ❖ Steadfast in the LIVING WORD

CHAPTER SEVEN   92
BE FRUITFUL IN THE WORK OF GOD
- ▣ The Great Commandment
- ▣ The Great Companionship
- ▣ The Great Commitment
- ▣ The Great Contribution
- ▣ The Great Commission

CHAPTER EIGHT   141
BE FURTHERED IN OUR WITNESS OF GOD
- -The Principle of Knowing
- -The Principle of Showing
- -The Principle of Growing
- -The Principle of Flowing
- -The Principle of Sowing
- -The Principle of Going

CHAPTER NINE   147
BE FORTIFIED FOR WARFARE THROUGH GOD
- ➤ The Association Principle
- ➤ The Armor Principle
- ➤ The Ambassador Principle
- ➤ The Army Principle

CHAPTER TEN   154
BE FESTIVE IN OUR WORSHIP OF GOD
- ✓ Praise God For Your Relationship
- ✓ Praise God For Your Regeneration
- ✓ Praise God For Your Release
- ✓ Praise God For Your Relocation
- ✓ Praise God For Your Redemption
- ✓ Praise God For Your ratification & Record

SECTION THREE
Principles from the Apostle's Proclamation

CHAPTER ELEVEN — 167
THE PROVISIONS OF CHRIST
- ❖ Kingdom Parentage
- ❖ Kingdom Potential
- ❖ Kingdom Promises
- ❖ Kingdom Purchase
- ❖ Kingdom Position
- ❖ Kingdom Payment
- ❖ Kingdom Pardon

CHAPTER TWELVE — 171
THE PREEMINENCE OF CHRIST
- ✚ Christ is Preeminent in Salvation
- ✚ Christ is Preeminent in Representation
- ✚ Christ is Preeminent in Creation
- ✚ Christ is Preeminent in Operation
- ✚ Christ is Preeminent in Reconciliation

SECTION FOUR
Principles from the Apostle's Predicament

CHAPTER THIRTEEN — 178
THE PRISONER OF CHRIST
- o A Prisoner of Appreciation (who now rejoice)
- o A Prisoner of Afflictions (my suffering)
- o A Prisoner to Adherents (for his body's sake..)
- o A Prisoner of Assignment (made a minister)

I dedicate this book to my loving Mother who has crossed the celestial shores and taken sleep in Jesus. I anticipatorily long for our reunion in the new heaven and the new earth, where we will ever be together and ever be with Jesus our Lord. I miss your touch, I miss your talk, I miss your tenacity. I long to hear you laugh and watch you eat. I wish you were here, but somehow, I know you're better-off there.

Elizabeth Oliver Taylor
November 15, 1944 - May 2, 2014

Introduction

I love nursery rhymes. I recently heard a nursery rhyme retold and it got me in touch with what really matters.

In the closing of one his sermons, Pastor Robert Smith Jr. of the New Bethel Baptist Church in Detroit said, "Humpty Dumpty sat on a wall. Humpty Dumpty had a great fall. All of the king's horses and all of the king's men couldn't put Humpty back together again. They called on the horses representing strength and they call on the men representing wisdom, but nobody called on the King." Smith said, "If you break down in life, call on the King!"[i]

That's what it's all about. Living on a Kingdom Level is about connecting with the King, calling on the King, confiding in the King, and committing to the King.

I'm praying that as you read this book, you would all the more see yourself as a kingdom-member, as a kingdom-minister, and as a kingdom-missionary. I pray that if you hadn't already done so, that you would join Jesus on your journey through life and come to know that you are part of a kingdom-movement, a kingdom-mission, a kingdom-ministry, and that you are to carry a kingdom-message. I pray that you develop a kingdom-mentality and begin to live according to the kingdom-mandates that are revealed to us in Scripture.

If you a professing Christian, I pray that you become a progressing Christian. If you are religious, I pray that you move from religion to relationship, from religion to relevance, and from religion to being a reproducing reproducer as a vibrant, vital, and victorious disciple of Jesus Christ.

We are going to journey through the first half of the 1st chapter of the Book of Colossians and discover some kingdom-principles, some kingdom promises, and some kingdom provisions.

There is a section called *Reviewing the Revelation* after the first section. I've provided some spaces for journaling as you process what you've read in this book.

I hope you enjoy the book, but it's not primarily written for enjoyment, it's written for empowerment. I'm not trying to impress you as a writer, I'm trying to impact you. I'm imparting the Word to impact your world. You will read a lot of Scripture in this book, because only the Word of God and the Spirit of God can teach you what you need to know to maximize the one life you've been given.

It is with great pleasure and great humility that offer to you some of the things I've learned about living a prepared life by practicing kingdom principles.

Reginald D. Taylor
September 16, 2014

Section One

Principles from the Apostle's Praise

Colossians 1:1-8 (KJV)
1 Paul, an apostle of Jesus Christ by the will of God, and Timotheus *our* brother,
2 To the saints and faithful brethren in Christ which are at Colosse: Grace *be* unto you, and peace, from God our Father and the Lord Jesus Christ.
3 We give thanks to God and the Father of our Lord Jesus Christ, praying always for you,
4 Since we heard of your faith in Christ Jesus, and of the love *which ye have* to all the saints,
5 For the hope which is laid up for you in heaven, whereof ye heard before in the word of the truth of the gospel;
6 Which is come unto you, as *it is* in all the world; and bringeth forth fruit, as *it doth* also in you, since the day ye heard *of it*, and knew the grace of God in truth:
7 As ye also learned of Epaphras our dear fellowservant, who is for you a faithful minister of Christ;
8 Who also declared unto us your love in the Spirit.

Take my life and let it be
Consecrated, Lord, to Thee.
*Take my moments and my days,
Let them flow in endless praise.

Take my hands and let them move
At the impulse of Thy love.
Take my feet and let them be
Swift and beautiful for Thee.

Take my voice and let me sing,
Always, only for my King.
Take my lips and let them be
Filled with messages from Thee.

Take my silver and my gold,
Not a mite would I withhold.
Take my intellect and use
Every pow'r as Thou shalt choose.

Take my will and make it Thine,
It shall be no longer mine.
Take my heart, it is Thine own,
It shall be Thy royal throne.

Take my love, my Lord, I pour
At Thy feet its treasure store.
Take myself and I will be
Ever, only, all for Thee.

-Frances R. Havergal, 1874

Introduction

It was said of Francis Ridley Havergal, author of this text, that the beauty of a consecrated life was never more perfectly revealed than in her daily living. She has rightfully been called "The Consecration Poet."[ii] That's what I long for, a consecrated life, a life totally abandoned to God, a surrendered life.

That's clear and covert in the Book of Colossians. There are clues to Christianity, guidelines to godliness, and keys to kingdom-living. In the first eight verses of the Book of Colossians there are some things revealed that should be basic to every believer. There are some things that every believer should build upon. There are some things that every Christian should be bent toward and bound by and these things are couched down in this opening passage of the Book of Colossians. Let's see!

As is his custom, the Apostle Paul opens this letter to the church at Colosse with a salutation. Believe it or not, there's always some subtle revelation in the salutation. Notice what he says when he opens the letter......

Colossians 1:1-2 (KJV)
1 Paul, an apostle of Jesus Christ by the will of God, and Timotheus our brother, 2 To the saints and faithful brethren in Christ which are at Colosse: Grace be unto you, and peace, from God our Father and the Lord Jesus Christ.

Chapter One
The Priority that is Revealed

"Paul, an apostle of Jesus Christ by the will of God"

The term used here "apostle" in a technical sense refers to the twelve that were with Jesus from the time of His baptism until His ascension and to Paul who encountered the risen Christ on the road to Damascus. But "apostolos" in the Greek, in a general sense means "one sent forth." Prior to going further in the text I want to inform you that all believers are to flow in the apostolic anointing as ones who have been sent forth by the will of God to do the work of God.

We are sent like Paul was sent. Paul was, and we are sent to help get people saved through Jesus Christ, help get people sanctified like Jesus Christ, help get people secure in Jesus Christ, and help get people serving with, for, and like Jesus Christ. Let's think about these four things in terms of them being a priority for those who live under the rule and reign of Jesus Christ.

The Deployment Principle *Saved People Are Sent People*

Sent To Help Get People Saved
Mark16:15-16(KJV)
¹⁵ And he said unto them, Go ye into all the world, and preach the gospel to every creature.
¹⁶ He that believeth and is baptized shall be saved; but he that believeth not shall be damned.

I mention the mandate recorded by Mark because he emphasizes the going, the gospel, and the guarantee. Mark tells us that Jesus commissioned and commanded the church to go into all the world. This suggests that we have been sent to our neighbors and to the nations. Not only do we see his emphasis on the going, but also on the gospel. It's interesting to note that Christ did not commission us to preach prosperity, preach business principles, nor preach happiness promises. Rather, He commanded us to preach the gospel. We will take up the gospel in more detail in a later chapter, but to say the least, we are to share the story of His conception, His compassion, His cross, His crucifixion, and His conquest over death and the grave. We have been sent to a lost world to tell them about His love, His life, and His liberation for their salvation and transformation. Mark emphasizes the going, the gospel, and the guarantee. Jesus declared that if one believes they shall be saved and if one does not believe they shall be damned. I'm motivated and mobilized by the message. All the persons you love; your mother, your father, your sister, your brother, your spouse, your children, your relative, and/or your friend are bound by this message. If they place their faith in Christ they go to heaven, and if they don't they go to hell. Allow that guarantee to propel you to share the gospel with as many people as you can and leave the results up to God. I can't emphasize it enough, we have been sent to help get people saved. The second way we identify with the Apostle Paul is that we've also been sent to help get people sanctified.

Sent To Help Get People Sanctified *(Col. 3:16-17)*[iii]

Sanctification has three phases. We have been sanctified, we are being sanctified, and we will be sanctified. When one is saved, he is saved from the penalty of sin, he is being saved from the power of sin, and when that Christian goes to spend eternity with Jesus Christ, he will be saved from the presence of sin. I'm making reference to this maturity in the middle, to this process of becoming more like our Savior and less like ourselves. When Paul exhorted the saints in Asia Minor, through Holy Spirit-inspired (that's applicable to saints of all time), to "let the word of Christ dwell in you richly," he was telling them and us that we must be sanctified in our heads. When he said, "teaching and admonishing one another in psalms and hymns and spiritual songs, singing with grace in your hearts to the Lord" he was telling them and us to be sanctified in our hearts. And when he said, "And whatsoever ye do in word or deed, do all in the name of the Lord Jesus, giving thanks to God and the Father by him" he was telling them and us to be sanctified in our habits. Friend, this text is written in the context of a local church. The members of the body of Christ were instructed to be full of the Word as individuals, to fellowship in the Word as an institution, and to follower the Word of God to be an influence in the world. We are sent forth into the world to be disciple-making disciples. We are to be growing in the likeness of Jesus Christ and helping others grow in the likeness of Jesus Christ. I will say more about this verse later in the book.

Sent To Help Get People Secure
Colossians 2:6-7 (KJV)
⁶ As ye have therefore received Christ Jesus the Lord, *so* walk ye in him: ⁷ Rooted and built up in him, and stablished in the faith, as ye have been taught, abounding therein with thanksgiving.
- *Secure By **Growing Down** (rooted)*
- *Secure By **Growing Up** (built up)*
- *Secure By **Growing In** (stablished in the faith)*
- *Secure By **Growing Out** (so walk in him; abounding therein)*

Friend, the Christian walk is a faith walk. We are saved by grace through faith. We grow by grace through faith. We are victorious over sin and situations by grace through faith. This passage tells us to have some omnidirectional-growth. When it says "so walk in him," it's telling us to grow-out. When it says, "rooted" it's telling us to grow-down. When it says, "and built up" it is telling us to grow-up, and when it says, "stablished in the faith" it is telling us to grow-in. Normally when we hear the word "secure" we think only about the assurance of our faith, but I believe Paul is also making reference to the affluence of our faith. We need to be stable, but stability comes through steadfastness. Our fellowship with Christ and with other Christians builds our faith and our fortitude. We have been sent to help other believers become more established in the faith. Paul was given to this mission. When Paul wrote to the church at Rome, he told the believers that he wanted to be with them and impart to them some spiritual gift, so that they would be established.[iv] He told the Christians at Corinth that I'm praying that you enriched by him and that you come behind in no gift.[v] He told the saints in Galatia to stand fast in their liberty in Christ and to not be entangled by the yoke of bondage.[vi] He told the recipients of the Book of Ephesians that I'm praying that God would strengthen you in your inner man by the Holy Spirit and that you would be rooted and grounded in love, and be able to fully know the love of Christ so that you would be filled with all the fullness of God.[vii] He told the saints at Philippi, I'm praying that you would abound more and more in knowledge and all judgment. I'm praying that you embrace and approve things that are excellent and I'm praying that you be filled with the fruits of righteousness, which come through your relationship with Jesus Christ.[viii] There are passages in each book that Paul wrote in the New Testament that can illustrate his commitment to helping others get secure in the faith. We must be equally committed. The last part of this priority that was revealed is that we have been sent to help get people serving.

Sent To Help Get People Serving

1 Peter 4:10 (KJV)
¹⁰ As every man hath received the gift, *even so* **minister the same one to another, as good stewards of the manifold grace of God.**

It's interesting to note that out of the four times spiritual gifts are numerated/listed in the New Testament three of those times were penned by the Apostle Paul. In Romans Paul teaches that God has given to every man a measure of faith or an area of spiritual gifting.[ix] In Ephesians Paul teaches that the edification and expansion of the body of Christ depends upon the effectual functioning of every member in the body.[x] In I. Corinthians Paul teaches that though the gifts are different, and the operations and administrations of the gifts are diverse, they all come from the same Lord, the same Spirit, and the same God. He also teaches that every person in the body is spiritually gifted for the benefit of the other members.[xi]

The Apostle Peter builds on this in his epistle and tells his readers and us that every member is to minister. Every believer is to be builders in the body. Every saint should be serving. Every person who has a relationship with God through Jesus Christ has been graciously gifted and good stewardship of those gifts is executed by serving other members of the body of Christ with and through your spiritual-giftedness. We have been sent to serve and to help get other people serving. Prior to moving to the next revelation in the salutation "The Process of Reproduction," let me encourage you to discover your spiritual gifts, develop your spiritual gifts, deploy your spiritual gifts, and demonstrate your spiritual gifts to and for others who may have similar spiritual gifts.

Devotional Thoughts

Chapter Two
The Process of Reproduction

"and Timotheus our brother"

The Discipleship Principle *Disciples of Jesus Christ, Raise-up Disciples of Jesus Christ*

<u>Paul led Timothy to a Decision to Trust Christ</u>
1 Timothy 1:1-2 (KJV)
¹ Paul, an apostle of Jesus Christ by the commandment of God our Saviour, and Lord Jesus Christ, *which is* **our hope; ² Unto Timothy,** *my* **own son in the faith: Grace, mercy,** *and* **peace, from God our Father and Jesus Christ our Lord.**

In my church tradition we use the phrase "son in the ministry." Paul used the phrase, "son in the faith." This phrase indicates that Paul led Timothy to place his faith in Jesus Christ. We have no direct reference to this, but Acts chapter fourteen records where Paul was preaching the gospel in the public square of the area where Timothy lived. From all indications, Paul won Timothy to the Lord, instructed Timothy from the Word, and trained Timothy in the ministry. Every believer should be given to this kind of work. We should be committed to winning people to the Lord Jesus Christ, instructing people from the Word of God, and training people in the ministry of our Lord Jesus Christ.

_____
_____
_____

The Apostle John wrote a whole book for the sake of causing the readers to believe that Jesus is the Messiah, Jesus is God in the flesh, and that Jesus is the only Way to eternal life.

John 20:30-31 (KJV)
[30] And many other signs truly did Jesus in the presence of his disciples, which are not written in this book:
[31] But these are written, that ye might believe that Jesus is the Christ, the Son of God; and that believing ye might have life through his name.

Paul Led Timothy to Development in Christ
2 Timothy 2:15 (KJV)
[15] Study to shew thyself approved unto God, a workman that needeth not to be ashamed, rightly dividing the word of truth.

Devotional Thoughts

In the passage above Paul told Timothy at least four things to do as a leader in the church. These four things should be practiced and taught by every Christian. Paul told Timothy to *be studious*. He said, "study" the term in the Greek means to exert diligence. It means to give one's self too rigorously. Every believer should rigorously read, research, reflect-on, and remember God's Word. And we ought to teach others to do the same. I'm a strong advocate of devotional-time. But, we not only need to be given to devotional-time, we must be equally given to developmental-time. We must put time in learning the Word of God. Paul told Timothy to *be stabilized*. He puts it this way, "study to shew thyself <u>approved unto God</u>." The believer must learn to live for the approval of God and God alone. We should live for the audience of One, for the approval of One, and for the agenda of One. Paul told Timothy to *be steadfast*. He says, "a workman that needeth not to be ashamed." The steadfast workman lives unashamedly. We ought to live with such a commitment to what God has called us to that we can come before Him and go before His people without shame. Paul told Timothy to *be standardized*. He said, "rightly dividing the word of truth." That phrase means cutting it straight. We must interpret the Scriptures correctly and instruct the Scriptures correctly. When we're reading, studying, discussing, and teaching the Scriptures, we must do all we can to find out what the text meant to the original author, what was understood by the original audience, and what the original message means for us today. We should be given to observation, investigation, interpretation, and application. In these areas and more we should be given to development in Christ. Growth is not automatic, you must consistently put in the work.

Paul Led Timothy to Disciple-Making for Christ

2 Timothy 2:1-2 (KJV)
[1] Thou therefore, my son, be strong in the grace that is in Christ Jesus. [2] And the things that thou hast heard of me among many witnesses, the same commit thou to faithful men, who shall be able to teach others also.

Many have made note of the fact that there are at least four generations mentioned in the above passage. There's Paul, there's Timothy, there's faithful men, and there's others. Paul was telling Timothy to stand on the truth he learned from him, then teach that truth and entrust that ministry to faithful men who would in turn do the same with others. This is discipleship. Discipleship is indeed becoming more like Christ. But it's more than that, it's helping others become more like Christ. Discipleship is believing in Christ, belonging to Christ, becoming like, Christ, bearing witness of Christ, and building others up in Christ.

Matthew 28:18-20 (KJV)
[18] And Jesus came and spake unto them, saying, All power is given unto me in heaven and in earth.
[19] Go ye therefore, and teach all nations, baptizing them in the name of the Father, and of the Son, and of the Holy Ghost: [20] Teaching them to observe all things whatsoever I have commanded you: and, lo, I am with you alway, *even* unto the end of the world. Amen.

I often say that the words recorded in Matthew 28:19-20 are the Master's last words, the Master's living will, and they ought to be the Church's leading work. I will develop this later, but for now, just let me say, no matter how successful we are, if we're not successful at being disciples who build disciples then we're not successful at being obedient to our Lord's command and commission. Let me encourage you to be a disciple-making disciple. Be a leader like Jesus Christ who raise-up leaders like Jesus Christ. Be a faithful follower of Jesus Christ who develops faithful followers of Jesus Christ. Be a student who imitates your Teacher and teach other students to imitate Jesus Christ the Master-Teacher.

Paul Led Timothy to Dedication to Christ
2 Timothy 2:3-4 (KJV)
³ Thou therefore endure hardness, as a good soldier of Jesus Christ. ⁴ No man that warreth entangleth himself with the affairs of *this* life; that he may please him who hath chosen him to be a soldier.

Devotional Thoughts

Dedication to Christ is marked by *endurance*. Paul told Timothy to endure hardness. Dedication to Christ is marked by *engagement*. Paul told Timothy to function as a good soldier who is at war. Dedication to Christ is marked by *exclusivity*. Paul told Timothy that a faithful soldier of Jesus Christ does not allow himself to become engrossed or entangled with the ways, whims, and wants of this world. Let's be dedicated to Christ and lead others to be dedicated to Christ. Let's endure our sufferings and situations. Let's engage in spiritual warfare and be ambassadors of Jesus Christ in the world. Let's live with exclusivity and not allow the mundane and mediocre distract nor detour us from the mission we've been sent on in the world.

Here are a few passages and points on being dedicated to Christ.............

Romans 12:1-2[xii]
Seek To Live A Life of
- *Appreciation* (by the mercies of God)
- *Presentation* (present your bodies)
- *Mortification* (a living sacrifice)
- *Purification* (holy)
- *Consecration* (acceptable unto God)
- *Dedication* (which is your reasonable service)
- *Separation* (be not conformed to this world)
- *Transformation* (but be ye transformed)
- *Reorientation* (by the renewing of your mind)
- *Magnification* (that you may prove what is that good and acceptable and perfect, will of God)

Hebrews 4:14-16[xiii]
Get Gripped By His Grace
- Hold on to your Heavenly Profession (v.14)
- Hold on to your great High Priest (v.15)
- Hold on through a Heart of Prayer (v.16)

Hebrews 12:1-2[xiv]
Feed & Fuel Your Faith
- Relish in Biblical Revelation (v.1a)
- Release the Bad that Ruins (v.1b)
- Run Boldly in the Christian Race (v.1c)
- Rely Heavily on your Redeemer (v.2)

Devotional Thoughts

Chapter Three
The Praise That Was Released

"We Give Thanks To God"

Colossians 1:3-8 (KJV)
³ We give thanks to God and the Father of our Lord Jesus Christ, praying always for you, ⁴ Since we heard of your faith in Christ Jesus, and of the love *which ye have* to all the saints, ⁵ For the hope which is laid up for you in heaven, whereof ye heard before in the word of the truth of the gospel; ⁶ Which is come unto you, as *it is* in all the world; and bringeth forth fruit, as *it doth* also in you, since the day ye heard *of it*, and knew the grace of God in truth: ⁷ As ye also learned of Epaphras our dear fellowservant, who is for you a faithful minister of Christ; ⁸ Who also declared unto us your love in the Spirit.

The Delightful Principle *Kingdom People Praise God For The People In The Kingdom*

Paul Praises God For Their Faith In Christ *(Since we heard of your faith in Christ Jesus)*
The Bible teaches about at least four kinds of faith. I understand and communicate Biblical faith in these four ways. There is saving faith, sanctifying faith, serving faith, and sustaining faith. The term used for faith "pisteouo" in the Greek means to be fully persuaded, to place full confidence in, and to unreservedly rely upon. Consider these four types of faith with me.

- Saving Faith: (***John 1:10-13***[xv]; ***Eph. 2:8***)[14]

Saving faith is exercised when a lost person places his or her trust in the Person and the work of Jesus Christ for their salvation. A simple way of explaining this is the ABC formula. Acknowledge that you are a sinner, acknowledge that God is Holy & Sovereign, and acknowledge that Jesus Christ is the Savior. Believe that Jesus Christ was conceived, that He was crucified for your sins, and that He conquered death and the grave through His Resurrection. Confess your sins and confess that Jesus is Lord. Now of course, saving faith requires repentance, but when one becomes aware of the fact that he and his sin is an offence to God and become aware of God's wrath toward sin and love toward the sinner, this produces genuine repentance in the heart of those who exercise saving faith.

Devotional Thoughts

- *Sanctifying Faith*

Romans 6:1-13 (KJV)

[1] What shall we say then? Shall we continue in sin, that grace may abound? [2] God forbid. How shall we, that are dead to sin, live any longer therein? [3] Know ye not, that so many of us as were baptized into Jesus Christ were baptized into his death? [4] Therefore we are buried with him by baptism into death: that like as Christ was raised up from the dead by the glory of the Father, even so we also should walk in newness of life. [5] For if we have been planted together in the likeness of his death, we shall be also *in the likeness* of *his* resurrection: [6] Knowing this, that our old man is crucified with *him*, that the body of sin might be destroyed, that henceforth we should not serve sin. [7] For he that is dead is freed from sin. [8] Now if we be dead with Christ, we believe that we shall also live with him: [9] Knowing that Christ being raised from the dead dieth no more; death hath no more dominion over him. [10] For in that he died, he died unto sin once: but in that he liveth, he liveth unto God. [11] Likewise reckon ye also yourselves to be dead indeed unto sin, but alive unto God through Jesus Christ our Lord. [12] Let not sin therefore reign in your mortal body, that ye should obey it in the lusts thereof. [13] Neither yield ye your members *as* instruments of unrighteousness unto sin: but yield yourselves unto God, as those that are alive from the dead, and your members *as* instruments of righteousness unto God.

Devotional Thoughts

The passage above teaches us that we are dead to sin, we are delivered in Christ, we don't have to be dominated by the flesh, and that we can live with dedication to God. Listen, the more Word you get in you, the more world you get out of you. The more you feed your faith through the Word[15], the more you starve your flesh and its ways[16]. I pray that you build-up and exercise sanctifying faith.

- *Serving Faith*

Matthew 4:10 (KJV)
[10] Then saith Jesus unto him, Get thee hence, Satan: for it is written, Thou shalt worship the Lord thy God, and him only shalt thou serve.

Matthew quotes Jesus telling the devil that it is written, "Thou shalt worship the Lord thy God, and him only shalt thou serve." I honestly believe that Moses and Jesus used the terms worship and serve interchangeably. But I also believe that if you worship God entirely, then you will serve God exclusively. I believe that if you magnify God in your heart, then you will minister for God with your hands. I believe that how you see God determines how you serve God. I praying that you get a fresh revelation of the Majesty of God and thereby become relevant in the ministry of God. One of the things I try to guard from as a preacher, pastor, and professor is, I want to make sure that I'm not loving what I do for Him more than I'm loving Him. I'm trying to be careful not to spend more time preparing my sermons than I'm spending preparing myself. I shouldn't and you shouldn't be more consumed with developing lessons than we are consumed with developing our lives.

The Apostle not only the message of sustaining faith but he provided a model of sustaining faith.

2 Corinthians 4:8-15 (KJV)
[8] *We are* troubled on every side, yet not distressed; *we are* perplexed, but not in despair; [9] Persecuted, but not forsaken; cast down, but not destroyed; [10] Always bearing about in the body the dying of the Lord Jesus, that the life also of Jesus might be made manifest in our body. [11] For we which live are alway delivered unto death for Jesus' sake, that the life also of Jesus might be made manifest in our mortal flesh. [12] So then death worketh in us, but life in you. [13] We having the same spirit of faith, according as it is written, I believed, and therefore have I spoken; we also believe, and therefore speak; [14] Knowing that he which raised up the Lord Jesus shall raise up us also by Jesus, and shall present *us* with you. [15] For all things *are* for your sakes, that the abundant grace might through the thanksgiving of many redound to the glory of God.

Devotional Thoughts

_____
_____
_____
_____
_____
_____
_____
_____
_____
_____

Paul's model teaches us that when we're focused on our Master, we're not frustrated with the ministry. When we're devoted to His agenda we're not detoured by Satan's attacks. In one sense Paul was saying, though we are walking through the valley of suffering, we are still experiencing the victory of our Savior. Hey listen, don't do ministry in the power of your flesh, do ministry in the power of your Father. Don't try to do His work without His Presence, His Power, nor His Precepts. Lean on God for serving faith.

- Sustaining Faith

I am told that Mother Teresa said, "faith keeps those who keep the faith." Wow! In the Bible there are several terms that refer to faith. You find words like remember, wait, trust, seek, call, and of course, faith.

Listen to David

Psalm 18:1-3 (KJV)
¹ I will love thee, O LORD, my strength.
² The LORD *is* my rock, and my fortress, and my deliverer; my God, my strength, in whom I will trust; my buckler, and the horn of my salvation, *and* my high tower. ³ I will call upon the LORD, *who is worthy* to be praised: so shall I be saved from mine enemies.

Psalm 20:7 (KJV)
⁷ Some *trust* in chariots, and some in horses: but we will remember the name of the LORD our God.

Psalm 25:1-3 (KJV)
¹ Unto thee, O LORD, do I lift up my soul.
² O my God, I trust in thee: let me not be ashamed, let not mine enemies triumph over me.

³ Yea, let none that wait on thee be ashamed: let them be ashamed which transgress without cause.

Listen to Solomon

Proverbs 3:5-6 (KJV)

⁵ Trust in the LORD with all thine heart; and lean not unto thine own understanding.

⁶ In all thy ways acknowledge him, and he shall direct thy paths*Proverbs 30:5 (KJV)*

⁵ Every word of God *is* pure: he *is* a shield unto them that put their trust in him.

Listen to Isaiah

Isaiah 26:3-4 (KJV)

³ Thou wilt keep *him* in perfect peace, *whose* mind *is* stayed *on thee*: because he trusteth in thee.

⁴ Trust ye in the LORD for ever: for in the LORD JEHOVAH *is* everlasting strength:

Isaiah 40:31 (KJV)

³¹ But they that wait upon the LORD shall renew *their* strength; they shall mount up with wings as eagles; they shall run, and not be weary; *and* they shall walk, and not faint.

Listen to Paul

1 Corinthians 16:13 (KJV)

¹³ Watch ye, stand fast in the faith, quit you like men, be strong.

> *Ephesians 6:10-13 (KJV)*
> ¹⁰ Finally, my brethren, be strong in the Lord, and in the power of his might. ¹¹ Put on the whole armour of God, that ye may be able to stand against the wiles of the devil. ¹² For we wrestle not against flesh and blood, but against principalities, against powers, against the rulers of the darkness of this world, against spiritual wickedness in high *places*. ¹³ Wherefore take unto you the whole armour of God, that ye may be able to withstand in the evil day, and having done all, to stand.

Wow! Those are some awesome verses. If you consistently allow God to speak to you through Scripture and you consistently speak to God through prayer, then you will develop and experience sustaining faith.

Paul Praises God For Their Fellowship In Christ *(and of the love which ye have to all the saints)*

Fellowship is not about just meeting, greeting, and eating. Fellowship is not something you can relegate to a room, a family-life center, a kitchen, a cafeteria, or to what we call a fellowship-hall. Fellowship happens when Christians come together, when Christians do life together, and when Christians meet needs together. We will discuss the dynamics of fellowship later in the book, but for now, let's just say, fellowship is about loving, living, and laboring together.

_____
_____
_____

Kingdom Christians Love Together

John 13:34-35 (KJV)
³⁴ A new commandment I give unto you, That ye love one another; as I have loved you, that ye also love one another. ³⁵ By this shall all *men* know that ye are my disciples, if ye have love one to another.

Jesus commands the disciples and us to love one another as He has loved them and has loved us. The fact that it's a command means that it is not optional. It is not up for debate or discussion. Love among the saints is the thing that sets apart from the rest of the world. Love for one another is the thing that makes the world want what we have, desire to experience what we experience, and long to know the sense of family that we enjoy.

Devotional Thoughts

_____
_____
_____
_____
_____
_____
_____
_____
_____
_____
_____
_____
_____
_____
_____

Kingdom Christians Do Life Together

Kingdom people don't just meet on Sundays, or on Wednesdays, or on whatever day/evening your church meet for worship, for prayer meeting, for mid-week service, or for Bible study. We do life together. Our society has become so detached and individualistic and sadly, this has become the characteristic of Christians and congregations in the West. The Biblical model shows us the people of God doing life together. We see this model as far back as the Old Testament. The children of Israel were to stay together, they were to worship God together, pray to God together, to seek God through fasting together, and to hear and learn the Word of God together. That's another book for another time. In the New Testament, we see how the first century churched functioned and fellowshipped. It is from this model that we should try to engage our lives and establish our churches. It may be impossible to do what they did exactly the way they did it. However, it is possible to find some principles and practice those principles in our current context.

Consider this passage with me.........
Acts 2:37-47 (KJV)
[37] Now when they heard *this*, they were pricked in their heart, and said unto Peter and to the rest of the apostles, Men *and* brethren, what shall we do? [38] Then Peter said unto them, Repent, and be baptized every one of you in the name of Jesus Christ for the remission of sins, and ye shall receive the gift of the Holy Ghost. [39] For the promise is unto you, and to your children, and to all that are afar off, *even* as many as the Lord our God shall call. [40] And with many other words did he testify and exhort, saying,

Save yourselves from this untoward generation. [41] Then they that gladly received his word were baptized: and the same day there were added *unto them* about three thousand souls. [42] And they continued stedfastly in the apostles' doctrine and fellowship, and in breaking of bread, and in prayers. [43] And fear came upon every soul: and many wonders and signs were done by the apostles. [44] And all that believed were together, and had all things common; [45] And sold their possessions and goods, and parted them to all *men*, as every man had need. [46] And they, continuing daily with one accord in the temple, and breaking bread from house to house, did eat their meat with gladness and singleness of heart, [47] Praising God, and having favour with all the people. And the Lord added to the church daily such as should be saved.

Devotional Thoughts

Luke tells us that on the Day of Pentecost Peter preaches the gospel and 3,000 people get saved. Then he shows us what they did. I think verse 42 is foundational and verses 43-47 if the fruit of how they functioned in verse 42. They continued steadfastly in the apostle's doctrine, they continued steadfastly in fellowship, they continued steadfastly in holy-communion, and they continued steadfastly in prayers. In verse 43 Luke tells us that the people around them reverenced the Church and that the apostles did many sign-miracles. He tells us in verses 44 and 45 that the believers were together and that they met each other needs among themselves. He tells us in verse 46 that they worshiped together and took communion together in both the temple and from house to house with gladness and singleness of heart. Then he tells that they were continuously praising God, they were having favor with the people, and that the Lord was adding to the Church daily people who were being saved. This was a vibrant fellowship. This was a close-knit and productive group of believers. The things they did and the way they did the things they did should guide what we do and how we do what we do in the 21st Century.

Consider the things they did together with me......
- ***They Regularly Received Revelation Together*** (they continued steadfastly in the apostle's doctrine/teaching)
- ***They Consistently Stayed in Community Together*** (in fellowship, they that believed were together and had all things common)

- *They Regularly Reviewed & Remembered The Redemptive Work of Christ Together* (in breaking of bread; breaking bread from house to house)
- *They Constantly Communicated With God Together* (and in prayers)
- *They Evangelized & Experienced Kingdom-Expansion Everyday Together* (Praising God, having favor with the people, and the Lord added to the church daily such as should be saved)

They were doing life together. We should praise God for the churches/Christians that are doing life together. If you're a leader of a church, please don't settle for business as usual if you and your people are not doing life together. If you are a member who is not connected to other believers in full and frequent fellowship, please get connected because your growth, the growth of others, and the expansion of God's kingdom in the earth depends upon it.

Devotional Thoughts

_____
_____
_____
_____
_____
_____
_____
_____
_____
_____
_____

Kingdom Christians Labor Together

Mark 2:1-12 (KJV)
[1] And again he entered into Capernaum after *some* days; and it was noised that he was in the house. [2] And straightway many were gathered together, insomuch that there was no room to receive *them*, no, not so much as about the door: and he preached the word unto them. [3] And they come unto him, bringing one sick of the palsy, which was borne of four. [4] And when they could not come nigh unto him for the press, they uncovered the roof where he was: and when they had broken *it* up, they let down the bed wherein the sick of the palsy lay. [5] When Jesus saw their faith, he said unto the sick of the palsy, Son, thy sins be forgiven thee. [6] But there were certain of the scribes sitting there, and reasoning in their hearts, [7] Why doth this *man* thus speak blasphemies? who can forgive sins but God only? [8] And immediately when Jesus perceived in his spirit that they so reasoned within themselves, he said unto them, Why reason ye these things in your hearts? [9] Whether is it easier to say to the sick of the palsy, *Thy* sins be forgiven thee; or to say, Arise, and take up thy bed, and walk? [10] But that ye may know that the Son of man hath power on earth to forgive sins, (he saith to the sick of the palsy,) [11] I say unto thee, Arise, and take up thy bed, and go thy way into thine house. [12] And immediately he arose, took up the bed, and went forth before them all; insomuch that they were all amazed, and glorified God, saying, We never saw it on this fashion.

Devotional Thoughts

This passage from the Gospel of Mark illustrates the power of laboring together. John C. Maxwell said, "Teamwork makes the dream work."[xvi] In the passage above four men carried one man to Jesus. One couldn't lift him alone. One couldn't leverage him alone. One couldn't rip-off the roof alone. But together they accomplished the task of taking this helpless man to Jesus. The Scripture says that when Jesus saw their faith (the faith of the four team-members) He forgave the man of his sins and then ultimately healed him of his condition. What a lesson for us! Together we can do more. Together we can accomplish more. Together we can win more lost people and make more disciples of Jesus Christ. World-evangelization is a team-mission that requires a team-mentality. Let's not be lone ranger Christians. Let's not do our thing alone. Let's not be so consumed with what we call "my ministry," that we never connect and get His ministry do. Let's labor together.

Kingdom Christians love together, do life together, and labor together!

Devotional Thoughts

_____
_____
_____
_____
_____
_____
_____
_____
_____

Paul praised God for their faith, for their fellowship, and also for their future.

Paul Praises God For Their Future In Christ (*For the hope which is laid up for you in heaven*)

If you are a believer in Jesus Christ I have three things I want to share with that God promises you in the Scriptures. Let me encourage you to take refuge in these revelations and share them with both the saved and the unsaved people in your life. We have been promised that we will *receive new bodies*, we will be *reformed into new beings*, and that we will *be rewarded new blessings*.

We Will Receive New Bodies
1 Corinthians 15:51-57 (KJV)
^{51} Behold, I shew you a mystery; We shall not all sleep, but we shall all be changed,
^{52} In a moment, in the twinkling of an eye, at the last trump: for the trumpet shall sound, and the dead shall be raised incorruptible, and we shall be changed.
^{53} For this corruptible must put on incorruption, and this mortal *must* put on immortality.
^{54} So when this corruptible shall have put on incorruption, and this mortal shall have put on immortality, then shall be brought to pass the saying that is written, Death is swallowed up in victory.
^{55} O death, where *is* thy sting? O grave, where *is* thy victory?
^{56} The sting of death *is* sin; and the strength of sin *is* the law.
^{57} But thanks *be* to God, which giveth us the victory through our Lord Jesus Christ.

We Will Be Reformed Into New Beings
1 John 3:1-2 (KJV)
¹ Behold, what manner of love the Father hath bestowed upon us, that we should be called the sons of God: therefore the world knoweth us not, because it knew him not. ² Beloved, now are we the sons of God, and it doth not yet appear what we shall be: but we know that, when he shall appear, we shall be like him; for we shall see him as he is.

We Will Be Reward New Blessings
1 Peter 1:3-5 (KJV)
³ Blessed *be* the God and Father of our Lord Jesus Christ, which according to his abundant mercy hath begotten us again unto a lively hope by the resurrection of Jesus Christ from the dead,
⁴ To an inheritance incorruptible, and undefiled, and that fadeth not away, reserved in heaven for you,
⁵ Who are kept by the power of God through faith unto salvation ready to be revealed in the last time.

We have hope beyond the grave. We can live life and face death because of our eternal security. Death is our greatest fear but it has been conquered by Jesus Christ. The grave is our greatest dread but it has been swallowed up by our Savior. Because He lives we shall live. Because he got up, we will get up. Because He is alive forever more, we shall be alive throughout eternity. Praise God for His promises!

Devotional Thoughts

_____
_____
_____
_____

Paul praised God for their faith, for their fellowship, for their future, and also for their fruit in Christ.

Paul Praises God For Their Fruit In Christ *(and bringeth forth fruit, as it doth also in you)*

Paul said that the saints and faithful brethren in Christ which were at Colosse had heard about their hope in Christ in the word of the truth of the gospel and that that gospel was bearing fruit in the world and among them. A life that has been and is being impacted by the gospel is a fruitful life. Kingdom Christians bear fruit that magnify Christ and glorify God the Father. New Testament Scripture speaks of fruit in the life of the believer in various ways. We should be bearing what I call *character-fruit, convert-fruit, contribution-fruit, connection-fruit,* and *continuing-fruit*.

Kingdom-Christians Bear Character-Fruit

Galatians 5:22-23 (KJV)
**22 But the fruit of the Spirit is love, joy, peace, longsuffering, gentleness, goodness, faith,
23 Meekness, temperance: against such there is no law.**
Devotional Thoughts

When we walk under the control of the Spirit and according to the counsel of Scripture, we bear these nine fruit in our lives. We increase in love for God and exercise love toward others. We have joy on the inside regardless to what's happening on the outside. We enjoy peace with God and experience the peace of God. We exercise longsuffering toward individuals who are hard to get along with. We become more and more gentleness toward others. We increase in benevolence. The more we learn about God, the more we trust God. We walk in meekness. Meekness is not weakness, it is strength under control. Meekness implies that we let God be God and trust that He causes all things to work together for our good. We develop and demonstrate temperance. Temperance is self-control. The victorious Christian is not ruled by his/her flesh, but rather by his/her faith in the Word of God and in the God of the Word. Let's examine ourselves today and see if we're bearing character fruit.

Kingdom Christians Bear Convert-Fruit

Matthew 5:13-16 (KJV)
[13] Ye are the salt of the earth: but if the salt have lost his savour, wherewith shall it be salted? it is thenceforth good for nothing, but to be cast out, and to be trodden under foot of men. [14] Ye are the light of the world. A city that is set on an hill cannot be hid. [15] Neither do men light a candle, and put it under a bushel, but on a candlestick; and it giveth light unto all that are in the house. [16] Let your light so shine before men, that they may see your good works, and glorify your Father which is in heaven.

I watched Bill Hybels minister the Word at the Hill Song conference in Sydney, Australia and he said, the local church is the hope of the world, and the hope of the church is its leadership." That's so profound to me. Listen, the world is not going to be changed through politics, through education, through the criminal justice system, nor by the legislative, executive, or judicial branches of the government. If the world going to be changed it's going to come through the influence and impact of the local church living and giving the gospel of Jesus Christ. Matthew's record of The Sermon on the Mount provides for keys from our King on expanding His kingdom in the earth. After speaking concerning the inner-being of kingdom-Christians in Matthew 5:1-12, He speaks to the influence of kingdom-Christians. I'm sure what He said has far more meaning and implications than what I offer here, but consider these four things with me.

- **We Should Be Salt That Sanctifies** *(Ye are the salt of the earth)*
- **We Should Be Disciples That Penetrate The Darkness** *(Ye are the light of the world...)*
- **We Should Be Lamps That Light The Way** *(it giveth light to all that are in the house)*
- **We Should Be Ministers Who Magnify Christ and Givers Who Glorify God** *(Let your light so shine that men will see your good works and glorify your Father which is in heaven)*

Kingdom Christians make a difference in the world. People are saved because they come in contact with kingdom Christians. Families are fixed, relationships are repaired, sinners are saved, and destinies are altered because they come in contact with kingdom Christians.

Kingdom Christians Bear Contribution-Fruit

Philippians 4:10-19 (KJV)
10 But I rejoiced in the Lord greatly, that now at the last your care of me hath flourished again; wherein ye were

also careful, but ye lacked opportunity. ¹¹ Not that I speak in respect of want: for I have learned, in whatsoever state I am, therewith to be content. ¹² I know both how to be abased, and I know how to abound: every where and in all things I am instructed both to be full and to be hungry, both to abound and to suffer need. ¹³ I can do all things through Christ which strengtheneth me. ¹⁴ Notwithstanding ye have well done, that ye did communicate with my affliction. ¹⁵ Now ye Philippians know also, that in the beginning of the gospel, when I departed from Macedonia, no church communicated with me as concerning giving and receiving, but ye only. ¹⁶ For even in Thessalonica ye sent once and again unto my necessity. ¹⁷ Not because I desire a gift: but I desire fruit that may abound to your account. ¹⁸ But I have all, and abound: I am full, having received of Epaphroditus the things which were sent from you, an odour of a sweet smell, a sacrifice acceptable, wellpleasing to God. ¹⁹ But my God shall supply all your need according to his riches in glory by Christ Jesus.

Many Christians quote Philippians 4:19. Often, we quote it out of context. In the context, Paul is telling the Christians at Philippi that he's glad that they began to give toward the ministry again. He reminded them that in the beginning of his ministry they were the only ones to give. He also assured them that he was mentioning money because he desired a gift, but rather he was mentioning money/support because he wanted fruit to abound toward their account for their investment in the gospel. Then he told them that his God would supply all their need according to his riches in glory by Christ Jesus. When we quote Philippians 4:19 out of context we're claiming the promise without practicing the principle.   The principle is this: God always supplies for those who are generous toward the gospel ministry. If you want to invoke the hand of God, invest in the help of God. If you want to live with the assurance of His supply, then give in the assistance of His service. Kingdom Christians bear contribution fruit.

Kingdom Christians Bear Connection-Fruit

John 15:1-8 (KJV)
[1] I am the true vine, and my Father is the husbandman. [2] Every branch in me that beareth not fruit he taketh away: and every *branch* that beareth fruit, he purgeth it, that it may bring forth more fruit. [3] Now ye are clean through the word which I have spoken unto you. [4] Abide in me, and I in you. As the branch cannot bear fruit of itself, except it abide in the vine; no more can ye, except ye abide in me. [5] I am the vine, ye *are* the branches: He that abideth in me, and I in him, the same bringeth forth much fruit: for without me ye can do nothing. [6] If a man abide not in me, he is cast forth as a branch, and is withered; and men gather them, and cast *them* into the fire, and they are burned. [7] If ye abide in me, and my words abide in you, ye shall ask what ye will, and it shall be done unto you. [8] Herein is my Father glorified, that ye bear much fruit; so shall ye be my disciples.

In John Chapter 15 verse one through sixteen, Jesus uses the term abide (or the equivalents thereof) twelve times. It's clear that the key to productivity is connectivity. Those that abide (remain, continue) in Christ bear fruit, bear more fruit, and bear much fruit. We must have a fierce loyalty to the spiritual disciplines of prayer and Bible Study for the sake of increasing and intensifying our intimacy with Christ. When we do this, we allow Christ to cause His life to flow through us. The connected life is the fruitful life.

Kingdom Christians Bear Continuing Fruit

John 15:16 (KJV)
16 Ye have not chosen me, but I have chosen you, and ordained you, that ye should go and bring forth fruit, and *that* your fruit should remain: that whatsoever ye shall ask of the Father in my name, he may give it you.

Devotional Thoughts

We have been chosen to be changed.[18] We have been chosen to be His children.[19] And, we have been chosen to be change-agents in the world. Jesus told the disciples (and us), that I have chosen you to bear fruit- to bear character-fruit, to bear convert-fruit, to bear contribution-fruit, and continuing-fruit. When I think about continuing-fruit, I think about a couple of men that God used to help shape me. Pastor Jerry Metcalf is gone to glory, but he was the man God used to preach the gospel with power and clarity on January 6th 1992, the day that the Holy Spirit broke through my cold, corrupt, and callous heart and saved me. Pastor Herbert Davenport was a great encouragement to me. He coached me and counseled me. He spent large blocks of time with me for the sole purpose of encouraging me. Pastor Davenport was the father of a young lady I went to school with. Dena and her friends knew I was thuggish drug-dealer and they couldn't believe her dad when he told them that Reginald D. Taylor was preaching at his church. He told me they said, "I can't believe Dog preaching." Pastor Davenport believed in my conversion and my call. He gave me an open door to his pulpit, he told me whenever I wanted to I could come preach at Shiloh Baptist Church. I preached for him more time than I can count and had the esteemed privilege of serving as a pallbearer at his home-going celebration. Then there's Dr. David L. Boyle Sr. Dr. Boyle met with me two mornings out of each week for five years. One morning he would teach me Biblical doctrines and the other we would dialogue through different books he had me reading. He would allow me to be with him and witness him serving his wife and nurturing his children. Boyle was doing life-on-life with me. He was disciple-ing me and I didn't know it. He helped shaped my Biblical foundation in a relational context. He honed the spiritual disciplines of reading, praying, and journaling. He taught me how to prepare and how to preach. He modeled for me how to love and how to labor. He showed me how to worship the Lord and work for the Lord. He exemplified what it meant to be sold-out to Jesus Christ, what it meant to develop my craft as a preacher, what it meant to be a servant-leader, and what it meant to be a disciple-making disciple. These men, Jerry Metcalf, Herbert Davenport, & David L. Boyle, they being dead yet speaketh because they influenced my head, my heart, my hands, and my habits. They have continuing fruit. They influenced countless others and we are a part of their legacy. Let me ask you a question for you to deal with in your spirit. Are you living a life that will leave a legacy that lifts people to be all they can be in and for the Lord? Kingdom Christians bear continuing-fruit.

Devotional Thoughts

Well, in this first chapter, we've seen the priority that was revealed, the process of reproduction, and the praise that was released. I pray that you live with the priority of operating in the apostolic anointing of living as one who has been sent by the will of God to do the work of God. I pray that you spend your life helping people get saved, get sanctified, get secure, and get serving. I also pray that you live-out the process and see the products of reproduction. I pray that you lead people to a decision to trust Christ, lead people to development in Christ, lead people to disciple-making for Christ, and lead people to dedication in Christ. I pray dear friend, that you release praise to God for those redemptive blessings in your life and in the lives of those around you.

Devotional Thoughts

Reviewing The Revelation

1. What does the word apostle mean in general and what implications do the general meaning have for your life?

2. What four things did the Apostle Paul praise God for concerning the Christians who lived in Colossee?

3. Should you offer God praise for these things in your life and/or in the lives of those you are connected with in the body of Christ? Why or why not?

4. What four types of faith are mentioned in chapter one? Briefly explain each type of faith.

5. How have you experienced/exercised each type of faith? What type of faith are you exercising/experiencing right now? Explain.

6. What is fellowship? How do you provide and experience fellowship? What passage(s) in the New Testament illustrate Biblical fellowship?

7. What three things should every believer be doing with other believers? Please list some other things that qualify as fellowship with other believers.

8. What does the future hold for the believer? What three things are we promised in Scripture? How does promises in Scripture concerning the believer's future in eternity make you think and feel?

   _____
   _____
   _____
   _____
   _____

9. Name some places in Scripture that teaches about being fruitful. What kind of fruit should Christ-followers bear? Are you bearing fruit right now? What areas in your life need developing right now?

   _____
   _____
   _____
   _____
   _____

10. What is the key to your fruitfulness? Explain.

   _____
   _____
   _____
   _____
   _____
   _____
   _____
   _____
   _____
   _____
   _____

Section Two

Principles from the Apostle's Prayer

Colossians 1:9-14 (KJV)
⁹ For this cause we also, since the day we heard it, do not cease to pray for you, and to desire that ye might be filled with the knowledge of his will in all wisdom and spiritual understanding;
¹⁰ That ye might walk worthy of the Lord unto all pleasing, being fruitful in every good work, and increasing in the knowledge of God;
¹¹ Strengthened with all might, according to his glorious power, unto all patience and longsuffering with joyfulness;
¹² Giving thanks unto the Father, which hath made us meet to be partakers of the inheritance of the saints in light:
¹³ Who hath delivered us from the power of darkness, and hath translated us into the kingdom of his dear Son:
¹⁴ In whom we have redemption through his blood, even the forgiveness of sins:

In chapter one, we looked the priority that was revealed. In chapter two, we looked at the process of reproduction, and in chapter three we looked at the praise that was released, now we turn to the prayer for reformation.

In the Apostle's prayer for the saints at Colossee we find some principles for our own progress. We discover some disciplines that will develop us into devoted disciples. We come in contact with some clues to construct us into committed Christians. We are given some guidelines for our growth and a blueprint for Biblical living.

In this chapter I want to talk briefly about seven things we can glean from the apostle's prayer for the believers he was writing to.

1. *Be Filled with the Word (v.9)* "filled with the knowledge of his will"
2. *Be Faithful in our Walk (v.10a)* "walk worthy"
3. *Be Focused on His Will (v.10b)* "unto all pleasing"
4. *Be Fruitful in His Work (v.10c)* "fruitful in every good work"
5. *Be Furthered in Our Witness (v.10d)* "increasing in the knowledge of God"
6. *Be Fortified for Warfare (v.11)* "Strengthened with all might"
7. *Be Festive in our Worship (v.12-14)* "Giving thanks unto the Father"

Chapter Four
Be Filled With The Word of God

"That Ye Might Be Filled With The Knowledge of His Will"

The first clue to being formed into a faithful disciple of Jesus Christ is being filled with the Word of God. Paul says that he's praying that they would "be filled with the knowledge of his will in all wisdom and spiritual understanding." If I can bag into the text, spiritual understanding (pneumatikos sunesis in the Greek) means clarity for the Comforter. It means an understanding that can only be produced through and provided by the Holy Spirit. Wisdom (sophia in the Greek) means the ability to regulate a relationship with God by the application of Scriptural knowledge. The word "will" (thelema in the Greek) refers to the patterns, the plans, the purposes, and the personality of God. I often tell people, you can't discover God's patterns, God's plans, God's purposes, and God's personality by reading the latest novel, by reading good self-help books, nor by reading the autobiographies successful, history-making human beings. You can only discover the patterns, plans, purposes, and personality of God by getting in the Word of God. Listen, God's Word declares God's will. God's Word describes God's ways. God's Word defines God's work.

The Devotion Principle *Growth Is Not An Automatic Process[xvii], Growth Requires Hard Work*

I want offer nine ways to get in the Word and get the Word into you. What follows is nine ways wo be filled with the Word of God. If you apply these things to your life, you will be formed into a faithful disciple of Jesus Christ.

Reading the Word

John 5:39 (KJV)
39 Search the scriptures; for in them ye think ye have eternal life: and they are they which testify of me.

Let me be clear, all Scripture points to Jesus Christ. If you read the Word and miss Jesus you have misread the Bible. The Scriptures are Christ-centered and centered on Christ. In order to know God, you must know Jesus Christ and in order to know Jesus Christ, you must read the Word of God.

I highly recommend Bryan Chapell's book: Christ-Centered Preaching. Chapell says, "Preachers determine the meaning of a passage by seeing not only how words are used in the context of a book or its passages but also how the passage functions in the entire scope of Scripture. An accurate interpretation requires preachers to ask, how does this text disclose the meaning or the need of redemption?"[xviii] Chapell holds that every expository sermon should point people to the Christ, to His unconditional compassion, to His redemptive cross, and to a confidence in Christ that brings conversion. All Scripture points to Christ! I can't overexpress the importance of reading the Word of God.

For more on reading the Word, I recommend to you Dr. Howard Hendricks's book: Living By The Book. He describes ten strategies of first-rate reading that will be helpful to you as you seek to read the Bible for all it's worth. Hendricks coaches us on reading thoughtfully, reading repeatedly, reading patiently, reading selectively, reading prayerfully, reading imaginatively, reading meditatively, reading purposefully, reading acquisitively, and reading telescopically.[2]

Receiving the Word

Romans 10:17 (KJV)
[17] So then faith *cometh* **by hearing, and hearing by the word of God.**

Our faith is formed and furthered by the Word of God. We are stretched and strengthened by the Word of God. We are encouraged and enriched by the Word of God. It is essential that believers avail themselves to receive the Word of God. Believers need to be receivers. When you consistently go to a Bible-study where the Scriptures are being rightly divided you are receiving. When you consistently participate in a small-group, life-group, or Sunday School Class where Christ is at the center and the Bible is the basis for instruction and discussion, you are receiving. When you regularly listen to tapes, CDs, podcasts, Christian radio, or watch videos/Christian TV programs through which the Word is going forth with clarity, correctness, and power, you are receiving. You must receive the Word to keep growing in the likeness of Jesus Christ.

Researching the Word

2 Timothy 2:15 (KJV)
15 Study to shew thyself approved unto God, a workman that needeth not to be ashamed, rightly dividing the word of truth.

The word study comes from a Greek term that means to exert diligence. It means to labor at. It means to work rigorously at discovering what the Word means. Believers must move beyond surface reading to responsible study. If you can't or won't go to school to learn how to responsibly interpret the Bible, then you must go to training and get some tools that will help you understand what the words in Scripture mean in the original languages, what the original author meant, what the original audience understood being said, and then discover what the passage being studied means for us today. There are several resources out there that can help you in this regard. Let me recommend Henry Virkler's book, Hermeneutics: Principles and Processes of Biblical Hermeneutics.

Give yourself to the study of God's Word. Receiving the Word is greatly needed but studying the Word for yourself is a nonnegotiable. When you receive the Word and can't review what you've received, then you have no way of knowing if you received the truth. Study the Word for yourself. Be careful not to study just to know the Word of God, study to know the God of the Word. The more you learn the Scriptures, the more you come to not only know about God, but also know God.

Reflecting on the Word

Psalm 1:1-3 (KJV)
[1] **Blessed *is* the man that walketh not in the counsel of the ungodly, nor standeth in the way of sinners, nor sitteth in the seat of the scornful.**
[2] **But his delight *is* in the law of the LORD; and in his law doth he meditate day and night.**
[3] **And he shall be like a tree planted by the rivers of water, that bringeth forth his fruit in his season; his leaf also shall not wither; and whatsoever he doeth shall prosper.**

The Psalmist opens the psalms not encouraging us to praise, nor to pray. Rather, he opens the psalms equipping us with principles. The first psalm gives us a formula for walking in favor. It gives us a blueprint for a blessed-life. In the negative, he says, watch your counsel, watch your company, and watch your conversation. All that is in verse one. But in verse two, in the positive, he says, work your contemplation. The blessed man delights in the law of the Lord and he meditates in the law of the Lord day and night. Reflecting on the Word is meditating. The word meditate comes from a Hebrew term that means to mutter and to moan, it means to churn and turn in your mind over and over again. Someone has said that worry and meditation is the same thing done with a different focus. Worry is focusing on and thinking about a bad thing over and over again. But meditation is focusing on and thinking about a good thing over and over again. Reflecting on the Word is churning and turning, muttering, and moaning, focusing on and thinking about Scripture over and over again.

Meditation is a mechanism and means of allowing God to speak to you throughout the day and provide illumination to the Scripture(s) you're thinking about. The person who watches his counsel, who watches his company, who watches his conversation, and works his contemplation shall be like a tree. A tree has *a solid foundation*. A tree planted by the rivers of the waters has a source of fulfillment. A tree planted by the rivers of the waters that brings forth fruit in his season has *seasons of fruitfulness*. A tree planted by the rivers of the waters that brings forth its fruit in its season and whose leaf does not wither has *a sustained fervor*. A tree that planted by the rivers of the water, that brings forth its fruit in its season, whose leaf shall not wither, and that whatsoever he doeth shall prosper has *a sovereign favor*. I want you to embrace and enjoy these benefits of meditating on Scripture. I want you to have a solid foundation, meaning that when the storms of life come you won't break. I want you to have a source of fulfillment that you will always be spiritually nourished and experience ongoing contentment and joy regardless of your outside circumstances. I want you to have seasons of fruitfulness where people will get regenerated, revived, and restored because of the influence that you have in their lives. I want you to have a sustained fervor so that you will never run low, nor lose your joy in Jesus Christ. I pray that you experience a sovereign favor where God blesses and makes successful everything you set-out to do. Develop a habit of meditating/reflecting on the Word of God.

Remembering on the Word

One of the most valuable things that Dr. Boyle challenged me to do was memorize Scripture on a regular basis. Meditation helps your walk, but memorization helps your witness. Meditation helps you focus on the Word, but memorization helps you feed others the Word. Meditation grips your head, but memorization grooms your heart. Meditation shapes your mind, but memorization shapes your morals. Meditation helps you in your hearing from but memorization helps you in your holiness before God.

Psalm 119:11 (KJV)
[11] Thy word have I hid in mine heart, that I might not sin against thee.

Our only hope for holiness is hiding the Word in our hearts. You can't stand against the World if the Word is not standing in you. The more Word you get in, the more world the Lord gets out of you. My Pastor, (Dr. Frank E. Ray Sr.) once said, "Being in the Word will keep you out of the world, or being in the world will keep you out of the Word." That's so true. You get the strength to stay straight from memorizing the Word. Building a reservoir of memorized Scripture enhances your spirituality in ways you can't imagine. When you remember the Word, you can recall it in prayer, you can refer to it when witness, and you can rejoice over it when worshiping. Friend, let the Word move from just being in your hand, just being in your hearing, or just being in your head and let it reside and resonate in your heart.

Reciting the Word

Psalm 119:43-48 (KJV)
[43] And take not the word of truth utterly out of my mouth; for I have hoped in thy judgments.
[44] So shall I keep thy law continually for ever and ever.
[45] And I will walk at liberty: for I seek thy precepts.
[46] I will speak of thy testimonies also before kings, and will not be ashamed.
[47] And I will delight myself in thy commandments, which I have loved.
[48] My hands also will I lift up unto thy commandments, which I have loved; and I will meditate in thy statutes.

Kingdom Christians declare the Word of God over every situation. There's nothing you will go through in this life that has not already been gone through and addressed in Scripture. Whatever challenge you need to meet, whatever change you need to make, or whatever charge has been mandated, the Scriptures speak to it. For every New Testament doctrine there is an Old Testament personification. For every principle in the Epistles there is a picture or parable in the Gospels. The Word has the solution to your problems, the answers to your questions, and the clarity to your confusions.

Devotional Thoughts

___
___
___
___
___
___

In the Old Testament, as long as the people were reading what God said, receiving, what God said, remembering what God said, reflecting on what God said, and reciting what God said, they were responsibly responding to what God said. But, when they slacked in the Word, they were slipped in their worship, and when they slipped in their worship, they became sloppy in their walk.

Examples, exhortations, and encouragements abound in the pages of the Bible. Devote to the Word, delight in the Word, and learn how to declare the Word. Paul called the Word of God the sword of the Spirit. It is the only offensive piece of weaponry mentioned in the armor. The word used for "Word" was rhema, which means a word from the Word. You must learn to defend yourself from the attacks of the devil, from the allurement of the world, and from the appetite of the flesh by reciting the Word of God when you are tempted, tested, and torn.

Reverencing the Word

Psalm 119:89 (KJV)
⁸⁹ **For ever, O LORD, thy word is settled in heaven.**

Psalm 119:96 (KJV)
⁹⁶ **I have seen an end of all perfection:** *but* **thy commandment** *is* **exceeding broad.**

_____
_____
_____
_____
_____

Psalm 119:127-128 (KJV)
¹²⁷ Therefore I love thy commandments above gold; yea, above fine gold.
¹²⁸ Therefore I esteem all *thy* precepts *concerning* all *things to be* right; *and* I hate every false way.

Psalm 119:160 (KJV)
¹⁶⁰ Thy word *is* true *from* the beginning: and every one of thy righteous judgments *endureth* for ever.

Devotional Thoughts

I perhaps should have dealt with this first, because how you see the Bible determines how you submit to the Bible. How you see the Bible determines whether or not you subscribe to the Bible. How you behold the Bible determines whether or not, and to what extent you believe the Bible. Here are some questions you need to wrestle with. Do you believe that the Bible is the Word of God? Do you believe that when the Bible speaks, God is speaking? Do you believe that there are no errors in the whole Bible? Do you believe the Bible is correct in its creation account, accurate in its historical information, trustworthy in its promises, true in its claims, and sufficient in its power? You must hold the Bible in high esteem in order to allow God to speak to and through your life. There's no middle road, the Bible is either God's Word or it's not. It is either fully truth or fully false. It is either informed by man or inspired by God. If you hadn't, settle the issue of how you view the Bible. Let me tell, the Bible is the Word of God. It is inspired by the Holy Spirit, it is inerrant, and it is infallible. The publishers of those pocket-sized New Testaments, has placed some powerful and precise things about the Bible inside those small copies of New Testament Scripture. Some anonymous genius wrote these words,
"THIS BOOK contains the mind of God, the state of man, the way of salvation, the doom of sinners and the happiness of believers. Its doctrines are holy, its precepts are binding, its histories are true, and its decisions are immutable. Read it to be wise, believe it to be safe and practice it to be holy. It contains light to direct you, food to support you and comfort to cheer you. It is the traveller's map, the pilgrim's staff, the

pilot's compass, the soldier's sword and the Christian's charter. Here paradise is restored, heaven opened and the gates of hell disclosed. Christ is its grand object, our good is its design and the glory of God its end. It should fill the memory, rule the heart, and guide the feet. Read it slowly, frequently, and prayerfully. It is a mine of wealth, a paradise of glory, and a river of pleasure. It is given you in life, will be opened in the judgement, and will be remembered forever. It involves the highest responsibility, will reward the greatest labour, and will condemn all who trifle with its sacred contents."

--Anonymous

Devotional Thoughts

Referencing the Word

Matthew 4:1-11 (KJV)
[1] Then was Jesus led up of the Spirit into the wilderness to be tempted of the devil.
[2] And when he had fasted forty days and forty nights, he was afterward an hungred.
[3] And when the tempter came to him, he said, If thou be the Son of God, command that these stones be made bread.
[4] But he answered and said, It is written, Man shall not live by bread alone, but by every word that proceedeth out of the mouth of God.
[5] Then the devil taketh him up into the holy city, and setteth him on a pinnacle of the temple,
[6] And saith unto him, If thou be the Son of God, cast thyself down: for it is written, He shall give his angels charge concerning thee: and in *their* hands they shall bear thee up, lest at any time thou dash thy foot against a stone.
[7] Jesus said unto him, It is written again, Thou shalt not tempt the Lord thy God.
[8] Again, the devil taketh him up into an exceeding high mountain, and sheweth him all the kingdoms of the world, and the glory of them;
[9] And saith unto him, All these things will I give thee, if thou wilt fall down and worship me.
[10] Then saith Jesus unto him, Get thee hence, Satan: for it is written, Thou shalt worship the Lord thy God, and him only shalt thou serve.
[11] Then the devil leaveth him, and, behold, angels came and ministered unto him.

Referencing the Word goes hand and hand with reciting the Word. I recommended reciting the Scriptures for the sake of strengthening your witness, but I'm recommending referencing the Scriptures for the sake of your warfare. I believe the passage above shows us how to defeat the devil and how to invoke angelic assistance. I think it shows us a glimpse of the fortitude that comes through fasting and praying. Jesus was able to withstand all three points of attack. The devil only tempts us in three places: the lust of the flesh, the lust of the eyes, and the pride of life.[3] He was hungry, so the devil attacked His flesh with an offer. Jesus quotes Deuteronomy 8:3. He was God in the flesh, so the devil attacked him in the area of pride. Jesus quotes Deuteronomy 6:16. Jesus was (and is) King of the earth, so the devil tempted Him in the area of the eyes. Jesus quoted Deuteronomy 6:13 & Deuteronomy 10:20. Christ exemplified for us the power of speaking the right precepts at rough points. When the devil tempts us we can reference and recite the Word to survive the lust of the flesh, the lust of the eyes, and the pride of life. I love the way that passage ends. It says the devil departed and the angels came and ministered unto Him. Friend, I challenge you to not only know the essence of what the Scriptures say, know exactly what the Scriptures say. Don't just know what you're thinking and saying is somewhere in the Bible, know where it is in the Bible. You can be faithful to God in combat, you can be encouraging to others in counsel, and you can be inspiring to followers when coaching.

Responding to the Word

James 1:21-25 (KJV)
²¹ Wherefore lay apart all filthiness and superfluity of naughtiness, and receive with meekness the engrafted word, which is able to save your souls.
²² But be ye doers of the word, and not hearers only, deceiving your own selves.
²³ For if any be a hearer of the word, and not a doer, he is like unto a man beholding his natural face in a glass:
²⁴ For he beholdeth himself, and goeth his way, and straightway forgetteth what manner of man he was.
²⁵ But whoso looketh into the perfect law of liberty, and continueth *therein*, he being not a forgetful hearer, but a doer of the work, this man shall be blessed in his deed.

Devotional Thoughts

_____
_____
_____
_____
_____
_____
_____
_____
_____
_____
_____
_____
_____
_____

When it comes to the Bible, teaching is for life-change. We learn the Word to live the Word. We discover what God's Word says, so we can do what God's Word says. Bible reading and Bible study is not just for information and inspiration, but primarily for transformation. Truth transforms. God didn't send His Word for us to just learn it and like it. He sent us His Word for us to live it. The Kingdom Christian is a Biblical Christian. The Kingdom Christian not only let the Word permeate his mind, but also purify his morals. James says that those who are hearers and not doers are deceiving themselves. When we know the way of the Word and don't go the way of the Word, we are like a person looking at his flaws in a mirror and choose not to fix the flaws. We are seeing what God says, but we are not being what God says. It's not about how many verses we can quote, it's about how many verses we keep. It's not about how many times we go through the Bible, it's how many times we allow the Bible to go through us. James says that the Biblical Christian is the blessed Christian. Let's make the commitment to be doers of the Word!!!!

I hope these nine disciplines become a part of your life. If you are already doing these things, stay faithful, stay prayerful, and stay encouraged!!!
Devotional Thoughts

_____
_____
_____
_____
_____

Chapter Five
Be Faithful In Our Walk With God

"That ye might walk worthy of the Lord"

Paul basically said, "I'm praying verse nine so you can produce verse ten." "I'm praying that you be filled with the Word, so you can and will be faithful in your walk." The term walk comes from a Greek term that means the whole round of an individual's activities. The term worthy (axios in the Greek) is where we get our English terms axle and axis. The word means of equal weight and balance. The word picture is that of justice scales weighing-out or weighing equally. Paul was saying that everything the saint does should balance equally with the goodness of God. That is, just as God has been immeasurably good to us, we are to strive to live good toward Him. Walk worthy. Let me give you these four principles on faithfulness before I move further.

The Deal Principle *Growth Equals Change, You Must Grow To Change & You Must Change To Grow*

- Faithfulness is *Required* of Saints
  Micah 6:8 (KJV)
  [8] He hath shewed thee, O man, what *is* good; and what doth the LORD require of thee, but to do justly, and to love mercy, and to walk humbly with thy God?

- Faithfulness is a ***Restrainer*** for Saints
Psalm 119:133 (KJV)
[133] Order my steps in thy word: and let not any iniquity have dominion over me.

- Faithfulness is a ***Refuge*** for Saints
Psalm 119:114 (KJV)
[114] Thou *art* my hiding place and my shield: I hope in thy word.

- Faithfulness is ***Rewarding*** to Saints
Psalm 19:7-11 (KJV)
[7] The law of the LORD *is* perfect, converting the soul: the testimony of the LORD *is* sure, making wise the simple.
[8] The statutes of the LORD *are* right, rejoicing the heart: the commandment of the LORD *is* pure, enlightening the eyes.
[9] The fear of the LORD *is* clean, enduring for ever: the judgments of the LORD *are* true *and* righteous altogether.
[10] More to be desired *are they* than gold, yea, than much fine gold: sweeter also than honey and the honeycomb.
[11] Moreover by them is thy servant warned: *and* in keeping of them *there is* great reward.

The Scriptures speak to how the believer is supposed to walk. I don't have all the answers, but I think I can outline some of what the bible describes as a walk that's pleasing to God. I now move from nine ways to be filled with the Word to eight ways to be faithful in our walk. I hope this encourages you to walk close to God, to walk clean before, and if you do that, you will hear clearer from God.

We Must Have A Faith-Walk

2 Corinthians 5:7 (KJV)
⁷ (For we walk by faith, not by sight:)
Hebrews 11:6 (KJV)
⁶ But without faith *it is* **impossible to please** *him*: **for he that cometh to God must believe that he is, and** *that* **he is a rewarder of them that diligently seek him.**

The Christian walk is a faith walk. Our salvation comes by grace through faith.[4] Our victory comes by faith.[5] Our growth comes through faith.[6] Faith is very essential in the life of the believer. The writer of Hebrews says that without faith it is impossible to please God. We must believe that God is who He says He is and that God will do what He says He will do. We must believe that He rewards our faith and our faithfulness. On this Christian journey sometimes you have to trust Him when you can't trace Him. Sometimes you won't be able to trace His hand, but you still have to trust His heart. You have to know that He loves you and that He's always working for your good and for his glory.[7]

Psalm 9:9-10 (KJV)
⁹ The LORD also will be a refuge for the oppressed, a refuge in times of trouble.
¹⁰ And they that know thy name will put their trust in thee: for thou, LORD, hast not forsaken them that seek thee.

We Must Have A Focused-Walk

Ephesians 5:15-17 (KJV)
[15] See then that ye walk circumspectly, not as fools, but as wise,
[16] Redeeming the time, because the days are evil.
[17] Wherefore be ye not unwise, but understanding what the will of the Lord *is*.

1 Peter 5:8 (KJV)
[8] Be sober, be vigilant; because your adversary the devil, as a roaring lion, walketh about, seeking whom he may devour:

The first part of the word circumspectly (circum) is where we get our English term circumference, meaning all around. The second part of that word (spect) is where we get our term spectacles, meaning to see or lenses through which we see. Paul was saying live with watchfulness. He was saying walk in awareness. Paul did not want his readers (and the Holy Ghost doesn't want us) to be unwise. Rather, He wants us and Paul wanted them to understand what the will of the Lord is. Kingdom people are focused people. We can't be oblivious to the corruptness of our culture, [8] we can't be ignorant of our inclinations,[9] and we can't allow ourselves to be sabotaged by Satan.[10] We must be careful and be prayerful as we seek to be in the world but not of the world.

Peter says that the devil is our adversary. The devil is dead set against us. The devil is relentless in trying to deaden, devour, and destroy us.

We Must Have A Free-Walk

To say the least, we are to be free from the contamination of sin, free from the condemnation of sin, and free from the control of sin.

Romans 6:1-13 (KJV)
[1] What shall we say then? Shall we continue in sin, that grace may abound? [2] God forbid. How shall we, that are dead to sin, live any longer therein? [3] Know ye not, that so many of us as were baptized into Jesus Christ were baptized into his death? [4] Therefore we are buried with him by baptism into death: that like as Christ was raised up from the dead by the glory of the Father, even so we also should walk in newness of life. [5] For if we have been planted together in the likeness of his death, we shall be also *in the likeness* of *his* resurrection: [6] Knowing this, that our old man is crucified with *him*, that the body of sin might be destroyed, that henceforth we should not serve sin. [7] For he that is dead is freed from sin. [8] Now if we be dead with Christ, we believe that we shall also live with him: [9] Knowing that Christ being raised from the dead dieth no more; death hath no more dominion over him. [10] For in that he died, he died unto sin once: but in that he liveth, he liveth unto God. [11] Likewise reckon ye also yourselves to be dead indeed unto sin, but alive unto God through Jesus Christ our Lord. [12] Let not sin therefore reign in your mortal body, that ye should obey it in the lusts thereof. [13] Neither yield ye your members *as* instruments of unrighteousness unto sin: but yield yourselves unto God, as those that are alive from the dead, and your members *as* instruments of righteousness unto God.

Paul teaches that we can be free *from the contamination of sin* because our old man was crucified with Christ. We were also raised to newness of life in and with Christ. There's something (Someone) in us that gives us the ability to grow in sanctification, to increase in holiness, and to say know to the flesh by faith.

Romans 8:1-4 (KJV)
¹ There is therefore now no condemnation to them which are in Christ Jesus, who walk not after the flesh, but after the Spirit.
² For the law of the Spirit of life in Christ Jesus hath made me free from the law of sin and death.
³ For what the law could not do, in that it was weak through the flesh, God sending his own Son in the likeness of sinful flesh, and for sin, condemned sin in the flesh:
⁴ That the righteousness of the law might be fulfilled in us, who walk not after the flesh, but after the Spirit.

We can be *free from the condemnation of sin*. Paul says that there is no sentence of death and damnation to those who are in Christ. He also says that we have something called "the law of the Spirit of life." That law works over the law of sin. The law of sin leaves you no choice, you must obey the dictates of the flesh because the unregenerate person has nothing or no one in him to help him resist. My Pastor used to say, when you're lost, you sin by force, but when you're saved you sin by choice because God has placed in you the power to overcome the sin in your life. We don't have to live like hell, live full of hell, nor die and go to hell. We are free from the condemnation of sin.

Galatians 5:16 (KJV)
¹⁶ *This* I say then, Walk in the Spirit, and ye shall not fulfil the lust of the flesh.

We can be *free from the control of sin*. We can walk in the Spirit. We can walk under the control of the Holy Spirit. When we live under the control of the Spirit we keep our flesh under subjection. The spiritual Christian is a Biblical Christian. He or she learns what the Bible requires and seeks the Spirit for the strength to walk according to Scripture. Paul said that when we walk in the Spirit, we will not fulfill the lusts, the passions, the desires of the flesh. In other words, we will be free from the control of sin.

We Must Have A Fruitful-Walk

Earlier we considered the different kinds of fruit our live should bear. We should produce character fruit (Galatians 5:22-23), convert fruit (Mark 16:15-16), contribution Fruit (Phil. 4:10-19), connection fruit (John 15:1-11), and continuing fruit (John 15:16). Here I just want to say to you, we must live in a way that we make our lives count for the Kingdom of God. Friend we have only one life to live and only one life to give. This is not a rehearsal, there is no second time around. We had no control over when we were born and we have no control over when we die. What we can control is what we do with time that we do have. Hey, don't waste your life, rather work your life for God. Serving the Lord is the best way to spend our lives! Notice what the Apostle Paul says in the book of Ephesians.

Ephesians 2:10 (KJV)
¹⁰ For we are his workmanship, created in Christ Jesus unto good works, which God hath before ordained that we should walk in them.

That term workmanship is poiema in the Greek and it means a hand-woven work of art. It's the term we get our word "poem" in English. You are a hand-woven work of art. God has been shaping you & God is shaping you into what He wants you to be. God is developing you according to His divine design.
- **God is Crafting You in His Sovereignty** *(we are his workmanship)*
- **God has Converted You in His Son** *(created in Christ Jesus)*
- **God has Commissioned You for His Service** *(unto good works)*
- **God has Called You for His Satisfaction** *(which God hath before ordained that you should walk in them)*

Dear friend, you were saved for service. You were made for ministry. You experienced a great conversion to engage in His Great Commission. You were redeemed to become a reproducer. You were selected by God to become a servant of God. God not only wants to work in you and work on you, but God wants to work through you. Let Him use you. Be His hands and help the helpless. Be His feet and go where He is not known. Be His mouth and share the good news of the Gospel. Be His shoulders and let some weary soul lean on you. Let Him use you. Let Him use you anytime, anywhere, and in any way He want to use you.

We Must Have A Fulfilling-Walk

Ephesians 4:1-3 (KJV)
¹ I therefore, the prisoner of the Lord, beseech you that ye walk worthy of the vocation wherewith ye are called,
² With all lowliness and meekness, with longsuffering, forbearing one another in love;
³ Endeavouring to keep the unity of the Spirit in the bond of peace.

Let me give you four exhortations from this passage.
- *Be Serious about the Business* (walk worthy of the vocation wherewith ye are called)
- *Be Sober in the Brain* (with all lowliness and meekness)
- *Be Sensitive to the Saints* (with longsuffering, forbearing one another in love)
- *Be Supportive to the Bond* (endeavoring to keep the unity of the Spirit in the bond of peace)

Dear friend, you must live to fulfill your call from God. You must live to fulfill your consciousness toward God. You must live to fulfill the compassion of God. You must live to fulfill the community of God (the church/body of Christ). If you lack in any of those areas, you will lack contentment and fulfillment.

Devotional Thoughts
_____
_____
_____
_____
_____
_____

We Must Have A Following-Walk

Ephesians 5:1-2 (KJV)
¹ Be ye therefore followers of God, as dear children;
² And walk in love, as Christ also hath loved us, and hath given himself for us an offering and a sacrifice to God for a sweetsmelling savour.

When Paul told the saints in Asia Minor to be followers of God, he used a term that means to mimic. It means to do what He does, to say what He says, to think what He thinks, and to do feel what He feels. Let me exhort you to do a few things.

- *Follow God in Closeness* (be ye therefore followers of God)
- *Follow God in Correctness* (as dear children)
- *Follow God in Compassion* (walk in love)
- *Follow God like Christ* (as Christ hath also love us)
- **Follow God through a Cross-like Commitment** (and hath given himself for us as an offering and a sacrifice to God for a sweet smelling savor)

We ought to live like Jesus, love like Jesus, labor like Jesus, lift others like Jesus, lead like Jesus, and listen to the Father like Jesus.

Devotional Thoughts

We Must Have A Fellowship-Walk

1 John 1:7 (KJV)
⁷ But if we walk in the light, as he is in the light, we have fellowship one with another, and the blood of Jesus Christ his Son cleanseth us from all sin.

Christianity is to be lived-out in community. We are to live with interdependence. Your spiritual growth depends on the model and the ministry of other believers. Your spiritual gifts are to be deployed for the spiritual growth of others in the body. We must not allow ourselves to be sucked into the individualism that characterizes our culture. We must stay connected to other committed believers so we can grow and flow according to God's design.

In the passage above, the Apostle John shows us at least three things we need in order to survive and thrive as Christians in this corrupt world.

- **We Need the Book** *(if we walk in the light)*
- **We Need the Body** *(we have fellowship one with another)*
- **We Need the Blood** *(the blood of Jesus Christ his Son cleanseth us from all sin)*

I'm sure John was speaking primarily of our initial salvation, but the principles also apply to our increasing sanctification. There is a place for being alone with God. Your time alone with God in His Word and in prayer is a nonnegotiable. However, you also need to be connected in community with other saints because God also matures us through fellowship.

Show me a person who thinks he can and/or tries to grow all alone, then I will show you an incomplete introvert. Show me a person who does not spend time alone with God in the Word and in prayer, but is always around other believers in the Word and in prayer. Then I will show you spiritually malnourished extrovert. If you are an introvert, you must set aside your comfort and connect in community with other Christians so you can be complete. If you are an extrovert, then you must develop the discipline of being alone with God. When you get alone with God and allow Him to speak to you through His Word and begin to speak to Him through prayer, you will grow much closer to God. Let your connection to Him be through your time with Him and not just with your time with others. Matter of fact, fellowship happens best when those who are fellowshipping with one another has been fellowshipping with God alone.

With that being said, get connected. Get connected to a Bible-based fellowship, to a Christ-centered fellowship, to a Spirit-led fellowship, to a discipleship-driven fellowship, and to a mission-focused fellowship. If you do that you will began to grow and flow on a kingdom-level.

Devotional Thoughts

We Must Have A Forming-Walk

Ephesians 4:17-24 (KJV)
¹⁷ This I say therefore, and testify in the Lord, that ye henceforth walk not as other Gentiles walk, in the vanity of their mind, ¹⁸ Having the understanding darkened, being alienated from the life of God through the ignorance that is in them, because of the blindness of their heart: ¹⁹ Who being past feeling have given themselves over unto lasciviousness, to work all uncleanness with greediness. ²⁰ But ye have not so learned Christ; ²¹ If so be that ye have heard him, and have been taught by him, as the truth is in Jesus: ²² That ye put off concerning the former conversation the old man, which is corrupt according to the deceitful lusts; ²³ And be renewed in the spirit of your mind; ²⁴ And that ye put on the new man, which after God is created in righteousness and true holiness.

This passage teaches us a few things about those who have not experienced regeneration in their hearts and therefore can't experience reformation in their habit,
- *Lost People Consciously Sin* (*the vanity of their minds*)
- *Lost People Are Constricted by Sin* (*because of the blindness of their hearts*)
- *Lost People Are Callous Toward Sin* (*Who being past feeling have given themselves over unto lasciviousness, to work all uncleanness with greediness*)

Saved people are different. Lost people consciously sin but saved people are convicted when we sin. Lost people are constricted by sin, but saved people are constructed to sin less. Lost people are callous toward sin, but saved people are in combat with their sin. What I'm trying to say is, on this side of heaven we will never be sinless, but since we're growing in the likeness of Jesus Christ, as time goes on, we are sinning less. The exhortation is this: Make Sure You Are Growing. Can you honestly say, I am closer to God today than I've ever been? Can you honestly say, I'm walking in more holiness today than I've ever walked in holiness. You should be growing closer to God and cleaner before. You should be putting-off the old man of your flesh and putting-on the new man which is after God created in righteousness and true holiness. I love the way Paul puts it in Romans 12.

Romans 12:1-2 (KJV)
[1] I beseech you therefore, brethren, by the mercies of God, that ye present your bodies a living sacrifice, holy, acceptable unto God, *which is* your reasonable service.
[2] And be not conformed to this world: but be ye transformed by the renewing of your mind, that ye may prove what *is* that good, and acceptable, and perfect, will of God.

Devotional Thoughts

Chapter Six
Be Focused on the Will of God

"Unto All Pleasing"

The Bible has a lot say about pleasing God. Consider a few verses with me before I offer you some principles on pleasing God.

Paul tells wives and husbands how to please God
Ephesians 5:22-27 (KJV)
22 Wives, submit yourselves unto your own husbands, as unto the Lord.
23 For the husband is the head of the wife, even as Christ is the head of the church: and he is the saviour of the body.
24 Therefore as the church is subject unto Christ, so *let* the wives *be* to their own husbands in every thing.
25 Husbands, love your wives, even as Christ also loved the church, and gave himself for it;
26 That he might sanctify and cleanse it with the washing of water by the word,
27 That he might present it to himself a glorious church, not having spot, or wrinkle, or any such thing; but that it should be holy and without blemish.

Colossians 3:18-19 (KJV)
18 Wives, submit yourselves unto your own husbands, as it is fit in the Lord.
19 Husbands, love *your* wives, and be not bitter against them.

Paul tells children how to please God
Ephesians 6:1-3 (KJV)
[1] Children, obey your parents in the Lord: for this is right.
[2] Honour thy father and mother; (which is the first commandment with promise;)
[3] That it may be well with thee, and thou mayest live long on the earth.

Colossians 3:20 (KJV)
[20] Children, obey *your* parents in all things: for this is well pleasing unto the Lord.

Paul says they preached the gospel to please God
1 Thessalonians 2:1-4 (KJV)
[1] For yourselves, brethren, know our entrance in unto you, that it was not in vain:
[2] But even after that we had suffered before, and were shamefully entreated, as ye know, at Philippi, we were bold in our God to speak unto you the gospel of God with much contention.
[3] For our exhortation *was* not of deceit, nor of uncleanness, nor in guile:
[4] But as we were allowed of God to be put in trust with the gospel, even so we speak; not as pleasing men, but God, which trieth our hearts.

Paul told the Thessalonians to grow in pleasing God
1 Thessalonians 4:1 (KJV)
[1] Furthermore then we beseech you, brethren, and exhort *you* by the Lord Jesus, that as ye have received of us how ye ought to walk and to please God, *so* ye would abound more and more.

John says prayers are answered when we please God
1 John 3:22 (KJV)
²² And whatsoever we ask, we receive of him, because we keep his commandments, and do those things that are pleasing in his sight.

The psalmist says that praise pleases God
Psalm 69:30-31 (KJV)
³⁰ I will praise the name of God with a song, and will magnify him with thanksgiving.
³¹ *This* also shall please the LORD better than an ox *or* bullock that hath horns and hoofs.

Solomon teaches that pleasing the Lord brings peace
Proverbs 16:7 (KJV)
⁷ When a man's ways please the LORD, he maketh even his enemies to be at peace with him.

The author of Hebrews says it takes faith to please God
Hebrews 11:6 (KJV)
⁶ But without faith *it is* impossible to please *him*: for he that cometh to God must believe that he is, and *that* he is a rewarder of them that diligently seek him.

Devotional Thoughts

I want to offer three principles that will help you be focused on God's will. I don't take this lightly because it's so easy for us to get distracted and detoured from the pursuit of pleasing God. Parents can get consumed with raising their children. Spouses can get consumed with pleasing and dealing with their spouse. Corporate and blue-collar workers can get consumed with doing their jobs. Insurance and financial brokers can get consumed with selling policies and enlisting self-motivated people. Educators can get consumed with faculty, staff, students, and lesson-plans. Children can get consumed with sports, music, and other extracurricular activities. Lord help us, pastors can get consumed with church buildings, church business, church boards, church budgets, & church battles. All of us run the risk of being consumed with something other than pleasing God and fulfilling His will for our lives.

No Word = No Focus
Little Word = Little Focus
Much Word = Much Focus

- ➤ Let The Word Govern Your Head (Deut. 6:4)
- ➤ Let The Word Govern Your Heart (Deut. 6:5-6)
- ➤ Let The Word Govern Your Home (Deut. 6:7)
- ➤ Let The Word Govern Your Hands (Deut. 6:8)
- ➤ Let The Word Govern Your Habits (Deut. 6:9)

Pleasing God is living according to the Scriptures

| The Dominion Principle | *Until You Make Jesus Lord Over All Your Life, He Is Not Lord Of Your Life*

2 Timothy 2:15 (KJV)
¹⁵ **Study to shew thyself approved unto God, a workman that needeth not to be ashamed, rightly dividing the word of truth.**
- **Be Studious In The Word** *(study)*
- **Be Stabilized Through The Word** *(to show thyself approved unto God)*
- **Be Steadfast For The Word** *(a workman that needeth not to be ashamed)*
- **Be Standardized By The Word** *(rightly dividing the Word of Truth)*

Psalm 119:105 (KJV)
¹⁰⁵ **Thy word** *is* **a lamp unto my feet, and a light unto my path.**
- *Mine The Bible* (Proverbs 2:1-6) *[Dig-up]*
- Memorize The Bible (Psalm 119:9-16) *[Dig-in]*
- Mimic The Bible (Psalm 119:133) *[Dig out]*

| Principles That Will Help You Be Focused On His Will |

Be Staying in The Literature of the Word

Be Studying The Lessons of the Word

Be Steadfast In The Living Word

Hopefully these principles will help you maintain a Kingdom focus.

Be Staying in The _Literature_ of the Word

The Bible is the greatest book ever written by all standards. The Bible provides every genre/every type of literature that has ever been read and written. Though it is not given to teach us history, the historical data is interesting, intriguing, and informative. The Bible contains prose and poetry that's engaging, enlightening, entertaining, and encouraging. The Bible provides great biographical and historical narratives. I love reading about how Joseph got in trouble because of a promise and how he went from a promise to a pit, from a pit, from a pit to an unknown people, from an unknown people to a place of prominence with Potipher, from a place of prominence to a prison, and from a prison to becoming Prime Minister over an unknown people. I love the narrative of Moses, how he was born during a time when the Hebrew babies were being executed at birth (full term abortion), how he was hid for three months, then placed in the Nile River, then found by his sister, adopted by the Queen of Egypt, and then raised as the son of a king. I'm always encouraged when I see that boy with a death sentence become the emancipator and liberator of his enslaved native people. Oh, there are so many more stories with which you can identify. Then there's the Wisdom Literature in the Bible. The Book of Proverbs is prolific with profitable principles for your progress. In the New Testament, the Gospels paint portraits of the kingliness and the kingdom of Jesus Christ, while the epistles provide principles for the subjects and servants of the King to live by. Then there are books like Daniel and Revelation that tell us what this world is coming to, how the devil, the dragon, the beast, the antichrist will be defeated by the Lamb, and how we will reside and reign with Him throughout eternity. Dear Friend, make the Bible your #1 read. Get more familiar with the Bible than you are with any other book. The Bible is God speaking to His people. Remember this, no matter what you hear from someone's speech or feel in your spirit, for it to be spiritual it must first be Scriptural. The Holy Spirit will not tell you anything in your bosom that does not line-up with what He has told you in His book.

Be Studying The Lessons of the Word

The Bible provides life-changing lessons from cover to cover. It provided lessons about family, lessons about faith, lessons about faithfulness, lessons about finances, and lessons about favor.

There are benefits of being in the Book
Psalm 119:97-104 (KJV)
[97] O how love I thy law! it *is* my meditation all the day. [98] Thou through thy commandments hast made me wiser than mine enemies: for they *are* ever with me. [99] I have more understanding than all my teachers: for thy testimonies *are* my meditation. [100] I understand more than the ancients, because I keep thy precepts. [101] I have refrained my feet from every evil way, that I might keep thy word. [102] I have not departed from thy judgments: for thou hast taught me. [103] How sweet are thy words unto my taste! *yea, sweeter* than honey to my mouth! [104] Through thy precepts I get understanding: therefore I hate every false way.

There are blessings for being in the Book
Psalm 112:1-2 (KJV)
¹ Praise ye the LORD. Blessed *is* the man *that* feareth the LORD, *that* delighteth greatly in his commandments.
² His seed shall be mighty upon earth: the generation of the upright shall be blessed.

There are blessings & benefits for behaving by the Book
Joshua 1:7-8 (KJV)
⁷ Only be thou strong and very courageous, that thou mayest observe to do according to all the law, which Moses my servant commanded thee: turn not from it *to* the right hand or *to* the left, that thou mayest prosper whithersoever thou goest.
⁸ This book of the law shall not depart out of thy mouth; but thou shalt meditate therein day and night, that thou mayest observe to do according to all that is written therein: for then thou shalt make thy way prosperous, and then thou shalt have good success.

The Demand Principle *The More You Grow, The More You Know You Need To Grow*

Be Steadfastness in The Living Word

Jesus Christ is the Living Word.[11] We abide in Christ by abiding in the Word. We hear the voice of the Living Word when we read the pages of the written Word. When you are focusing on the model, the ministry, the miracles, the mind, messianic-fulfillment, the message, the mercy, and the mandates of Christ, you are focusing on God's will.

Chapter Seven
Be Fruitful in the Work of God

"being fruitful in every good work"

I strongly believe and I strategically teach that every member is a minister. Every saint is supposed to be serving. Every child of God is supposed to be a change-agent for God. We are anointed ambassadors, we are royal representatives, and we are sent-out soldiers of our Lord Jesus Christ.

Like many others, I've tried to explain what every saint should be doing by packaging some passages so that they would be palatable and portable. I want to offer to you five great statements from the New Testament. I want to offer five statements and standards that were issued by our Lord Jesus Christ. I believe, the Christian that does these things are the Christian that's fruitful in the work of the Lord. Think with me about what I call Kingdom Purposes for Kingdom People.

- The Great Commandment: Matt. 22:37-40
- The Great Companionship: John 13:34-35
- The Great Commitment: Luke 9:23
- The Great Contribution: Matt. 25:31-46
- The Great Commission: Matt. 28:18-20

The Great Commandment

Matthew 22:37-40 (KJV)
37 Jesus said unto him, Thou shalt love the Lord thy God with all thy heart, and with all thy soul, and with all thy mind.
38 This is the first and great commandment.
39 And the second *is* like unto it, Thou shalt love thy neighbour as thyself.
40 On these two commandments hang all the law and the prophets.

The faithful, the focused, and the fruitful Christian is the Christian who loves God. I'm afraid that we've downplayed the term and the concept of love so much, that we tend love God like we want to and when we want to. The term used in the text "Agape" carries the connotations of being not only unconditional, but also unlimited. It's the kind of love that would do whatever to please its object of affection. This becomes challenging when you think about it in light of pet-sins. Do you love God enough not to gamble at the Casino or play the state lottery. Do you love God enough not to smoke cigarettes or totally abstain from alcoholic beverages, even though you say or you know you are not an alcoholic. Small stuff, I know, but do you love God enough to abstain from sexual immorality, or from stealing, or from cheating on your taxes. What I'm trying to get you to see is that the kind of love that Jesus was talking about permeates our being and penetrates our behavior. Notice three things about this kind of love.

- Our Love is to be…….
- **–To the Heavenly Father** *(Thou shalt love the Lord thy God)*
- **–Totally Holistic** *(with all thy heart, and with all thy soul, and with all thy mind)*
- **–Toward other Human-Beings** *(thou shalt love thy neighbor as thyself)*

If you don't already have it, ask God to give you a Great Commitment to the Great Commandment.

The Great Companionship

John 13:34-35 (KJV)
34 A new commandment I give unto you, That ye love one another; as I have loved you, that ye also love one another.
35 By this shall all *men* know that ye are my disciples, if ye have love one to another.

If you check it, you will find that the faithful, the focused, and the fruitful, manifests their love for through their love for other human beings. Listen there's no place for discrimination in the kingdom of God. There's no place for sizing people up or talking people down in the kingdom of God. There's no place for prejudice or preferential treatment in the kingdom of God. There's no place for racism, classism, nepotism, or any other ism the kingdom of God. The love that we are resourced to have and required to give is to be influencing every believer and initiated by every believer. We are to be ever-flowing channels of His love.

> - We Have Received Instructions from Jesus
>   –(a new commandment)
> - We Must Reform Into Imitators of Jesus
>   –(as I have loved you)
> - We Should Be Readily Identified with Jesus
>   –(by this shall all men know..)

We have received instructions from the Lord Jesus Christ. We don't have the luxury of not loving another believer because they are unloving, we've been instructed to love. This is a command, it's not optional, it's not situational, and it's not negotiable. It is imperative that we obey the imperative.

We must be reformed into imitators of Jesus. In and of ourselves we can't love each other like Jesus loves us, but we can allow Jesus to love through us. One of the things I do when I'm tempted to be unforgiving, harbor resentment, or tempted to not initiate reconciliation, I think of all the offenses God has forgiven me of and that propels me to forgive, to release, and to initiate reconciliation. God is making us, God is reforming us, God is conforming us into the likeness of Christ and the more we become like Him, the more we can love one another as Christ loves us.

We should be readily identified with Christ. I'm saying that when the world sees us they should be able to say, those are kingdom people, those are Christian people, and/or those are God's people.

Let me give you A Word ↓
- "from The Christ" on Companionship
- "from The Creator" on Companionship
- "on The Consecration" of Companionship &
- "on The Constancy" of Companionship

•*A Word From The Christ of Christianity*
John 15:9-17 (KJV)
9 As the Father hath loved me, so have I loved you: continue ye in my love. 10 If ye keep my commandments, ye shall abide in my love; even as I have kept my Father's commandments, and abide in his love. 11 These things have I spoken unto you, that my joy might remain in you, and that your joy might be full. 12 This is my commandment, That ye love one another, as I have loved you. 13 Greater love hath no man than this, that a man lay down his life for his friends. 14 Ye are my friends, if ye do whatsoever I command you. 15 Henceforth I call you not servants; for the servant knoweth not what his lord doeth: but I have called you friends; for all things that I have heard of my Father I have made known unto you. 16 Ye have not chosen me, but I have chosen you, and ordained you, that ye should go and bring forth fruit, and that your fruit should remain: that whatsoever ye shall ask of the Father in my name, he may give it you. 17 These things I command you, that ye love one another.

•*A Word From The Creator of Christianity*
1 Thessalonians 4:9 (KJV)
9 But as touching brotherly love ye need not that I write unto you: for ye yourselves are taught of God to love one another.

•*A Word On The Consecration of Christianity*
1 Peter 1:22 (KJV)
22 Seeing ye have purified your souls in obeying the truth through the Spirit unto unfeigned love of the brethren, see that ye love one another with a pure heart fervently:

•*A Word On The Constant of Christianity*
1 John 3:11 (KJV)
11 For this is the message that ye heard from the beginning, that we should love one another.

In Romans 15 the Apostle Paul speaks to us about....
–"Relieving & Receiving" & "Edification for Glorification"
Romans 15:1-7 (KJV)
1 We then that are strong ought to bear the infirmities of the weak, and not to please ourselves. 2 Let every one of us please his neighbour for his good to edification. 3 For even Christ pleased not himself; but, as it is written, The reproaches of them that reproached thee fell on me. 4 For whatsoever things were written aforetime were written for our learning, that we through patience and comfort of the scriptures might have hope. 5 Now the God of patience and consolation grant you to be likeminded one toward another according to Christ Jesus: 6 That ye may with one mind and one mouth glorify God, even the Father of our Lord Jesus Christ. 7 Wherefore receive ye one another, as Christ also received us to the glory of God.

In Ephesians 5 the Apostle Paul speaks to us about......
-*"Being Faithful Followers & Being Satisfying Sacrifices"*
Ephesians 5:1-2 (KJV)
1 Be ye therefore followers of God, as dear children; 2 And walk in love, as Christ also hath loved us, and hath given himself for us an offering and a sacrifice to God for a sweetsmelling savour.

In First John 3 The aged Apostle John speaks to us about......
-*"Your Sacrifice, Your Substance, & Your Service"*
1 John 3:16-19 (KJV)
16 Hereby perceive we the love of God, because he laid down his life for us: and we ought to lay down our lives for the brethren. 17 But whoso hath this world's good, and seeth his brother have need, and shutteth up his bowels of compassion from him, how dwelleth the love of God in him? 18 My little children, let us not love in word, neither in tongue; but in deed and in truth. 19 And hereby we know that we are of the truth, and shall assure our hearts before him.

People will not know that we a devoted disciples of Jesus Christ by our cars, our cash, our commodities, our cathedrals, our crowds, nor by our connections. People will identify us as disciples of Jesus Christ only if we love one another as He has loved us.

The Great Commitment

Luke 9:23 (KJV)
²³ And he said to *them* all, If any *man* will come after me, let him deny himself, and take up his cross daily, and follow me.

- **Come After Christ** *(if any man come after me)*
- **Come with Abandonment to Christ** *(he must first deny himself)*
- **Come in spite of Afflictions for Christ** *(take up his cross)*
- **Come with Allegiance to Christ** *(and follow me)*

This is a small passage that packs a large punch. This passage and others outline what Deitrich Bonhoffer calls the cost of discipleship. God invites and calls us to self-denial, to sacrifice, to suffering, and to continuous surrender.

When Christ said, "if any man," He made it clear that this requirement, this standard, and this stipulation applies to all who would want to become His disciples. Everyone who wants to follow Him must follow Him on His terms. He requires total sacrifice, total surrender, and total submission. Jesus is Lord, the question is, is Jesus Lord of your life, is Jesus Lord of my life? Well, Jesus is either Lord of all or He is not Lord at all.

Look at a few of those passages with me.

Luke 14:26-35 (KJV)
²⁶ If any *man* come to me, and hate not his father, and mother, and wife, and children, and brethren, and sisters, yea, and his own life also, he cannot be my disciple.
²⁷ And whosoever doth not bear his cross, and come after me, cannot be my disciple.
²⁸ For which of you, intending to build a tower, sitteth not down first, and counteth the cost, whether he have *sufficient* to finish *it*?
²⁹ Lest haply, after he hath laid the foundation, and is not able to finish *it*, all that behold *it* begin to mock him,
³⁰ Saying, This man began to build, and was not able to finish.
³¹ Or what king, going to make war against another king, sitteth not down first, and consulteth whether he be able with ten thousand to meet him that cometh against him with twenty thousand?
³² Or else, while the other is yet a great way off, he sendeth an ambassage, and desireth conditions of peace.
³³ So likewise, whosoever he be of you that forsaketh not all that he hath, he cannot be my disciple.
³⁴ Salt *is* good: but if the salt have lost his savour, wherewith shall it be seasoned?
³⁵ It is neither fit for the land, nor yet for the dunghill; *but* men cast it out. He that hath ears to hear, let him hear.

Devotional Thoughts

In the passage above, Luke shows us the requirements. But, in the passage beneath, Mark shows us the requirements and the rewards of forsaking everything and everyone to follow Jesus.

Mark 10:17-28 (KJV)
[17] And when he was gone forth into the way, there came one running, and kneeled to him, and asked him, Good Master, what shall I do that I may inherit eternal life? [18] And Jesus said unto him, Why callest thou me good? *there is* none good but one, *that is*, God. [19] Thou knowest the commandments, Do not commit adultery, Do not kill, Do not steal, Do not bear false witness, Defraud not, Honour thy father and mother. [20] And he answered and said unto him, Master, all these have I observed from my youth. [21] Then Jesus beholding him loved him, and said unto him, One thing thou lackest: go thy way, sell whatsoever thou hast, and give to the poor, and thou shalt have treasure in heaven: and come, take up the cross, and follow me. [22] And he was sad at that saying, and went away grieved: for he had great possessions. [23] And Jesus looked round about, and saith unto his disciples, How hardly shall they that have riches enter into the kingdom of God! [24] And the disciples were astonished at his words. But Jesus answereth again, and saith unto them, Children, how hard is it for them that trust in riches to enter into the kingdom of God! [25] It is easier for a camel to go through the eye of a needle, than for a rich man to enter into the kingdom of God. [26] And they were astonished out of measure, saying among themselves, Who then can be saved? [27] And Jesus looking upon them saith, With men *it is* impossible, but not with God: for with God

all things are possible. ²⁸ Then Peter began to say unto him, Lo, we have left all, and have followed thee. ²⁹ And Jesus answered and said, Verily I say unto you, There is no man that hath left house, or brethren, or sisters, or father, or mother, or wife, or children, or lands, for my sake, and the gospel's, ³⁰ But he shall receive an hundredfold now in this time, houses, and brethren, and sisters, and mothers, and children, and lands, with persecutions; and in the world to come eternal life. ³¹ But many *that are* first shall be last; and the last first.

- We Must *Come After* Christ (I. Chron. 16:11)
- We Must *Come With Abandonment* To Christ (II. Chron. 7:14)
- We Must *Come In Spite of Afflictions* For Christ (I. Pet. 1:3-9)
- We Must *Come With Allegiance* To Christ (Matthew 4:10)

Consider with me a few things that God wants from you.
–Your Sanctification & Your Witness
John 17:17-26 (KJV)
¹⁷ **Sanctify them through thy truth: thy word is truth.** ¹⁸ **As thou hast sent me into the world, even so have I also sent them into the world.** ¹⁹ **And for their sakes I sanctify myself, that they also might be sanctified through the truth.** ²⁰ **Neither pray I for these alone, but for them also which shall believe on me through their word;** ²¹ **That they all may be one; as thou, Father, art in me, and I in thee, that they also may be one in us: that the world may believe that thou hast sent me.** ²² **And the glory which**

thou gavest me I have given them; that they may be one, even as we are one: ^{23} I in them, and thou in me, that they may be made perfect in one; and that the world may know that thou hast sent me, and hast loved them, as thou hast loved me. ^{24} Father, I will that they also, whom thou hast given me, be with me where I am; that they may behold my glory, which thou hast given me: for thou lovedst me before the foundation of the world. ^{25} O righteous Father, the world hath not known thee: but I have known thee, and these have known that thou hast sent me. ^{26} And I have declared unto them thy name, and will declare it: that the love wherewith thou hast loved me may be in them, and I in them.

–*Your Service & Your Walk*
Galatians 5:13-14 (KJV)
^{13} For, brethren, ye have been called unto liberty; only use not liberty for an occasion to the flesh, but by love serve one another. ^{14} For all the law is fulfilled in one word, even in this; Thou shalt love thy neighbour as thyself.

Ephesians 4:1-3 (KJV)
^{1} I therefore, the prisoner of the Lord, beseech you that ye walk worthy of the vocation wherewith ye are called, ^{2} With all lowliness and meekness, with longsuffering, forbearing one another in love; ^{3} Endeavouring to keep the unity of the Spirit in the bond of peace.

–*Your Surrender & Your Worship*
Colossians 3:12-17 (KJV)
^{12} Put on therefore, as the elect of God, holy and beloved, bowels of mercies, kindness, humbleness of mind, meekness, longsuffering; ^{13} Forbearing one another, and

forgiving one another, if any man have a quarrel against any: even as Christ forgave you, so also do ye. [14] And above all these things put on charity, which is the bond of perfectness. [15] And let the peace of God rule in your hearts, to the which also ye are called in one body; and be ye thankful. [16] Let the word of Christ dwell in you richly in all wisdom; teaching and admonishing one another in psalms and hymns and spiritual songs, singing with grace in your hearts to the Lord. [17] And whatsoever ye do in word or deed, do all in the name of the Lord Jesus, giving thanks to God and the Father by him.

Come With Allegiance To Christ *(Follow me)*

My dears, you ought not try to function for Christ if you are not following after Christ. You will never fruitful in His work, if you are not faithful in your walk. You cannot fulfill the Word without following the Word.

- **Stay Connected To The Vine:**

John 15:1-11

[1] I am the true vine, and my Father is the husbandman. [2] Every branch in me that beareth not fruit he taketh away: and every *branch* that beareth fruit, he purgeth it, that it may bring forth more fruit. [3] Now ye are clean through the word which I have spoken unto you. [4] Abide in me, and I in you. As the branch cannot bear fruit of itself, except it abide in the vine; no more can ye, except ye abide in me. [5] I am the vine, ye *are* the branches: He that abideth in me, and I in him, the same bringeth forth much fruit: for without me ye can do nothing. [6] If a man abide not in me, he is cast

forth as a branch, and is withered; and men gather them, and cast *them* into the fire, and they are burned. ⁷ If ye abide in me, and my words abide in you, ye shall ask what ye will, and it shall be done unto you. ⁸ Herein is my Father glorified, that ye bear much fruit; so shall ye be my disciples. ⁹ As the Father hath loved me, so have I loved you: continue ye in my love. ¹⁰ If ye keep my commandments, ye shall abide in my love; even as I have kept my Father's commandments, and abide in his love. ¹¹ These things have I spoken unto you, that my joy might remain in you, and *that* your joy might be full.

- Stay Confident In His Voice:

Psalm 119:17-19 (KJV)

¹⁷ Deal bountifully with thy servant, *that* I may live, and keep thy word. ¹⁸ Open thou mine eyes, that I may behold wondrous things out of thy law. ¹⁹ I *am* a stranger in the earth: hide not thy commandments from me. *We need LEADERSHIP from the Word!*

Psalm 119:105 (KJV)

¹⁰⁵ Thy word *is* a lamp unto my feet, and a light unto my path. *We need LIGHT from the Word!*

Psalm 119:133 (KJV)

¹³³ Order my steps in thy word: and let not any iniquity have dominion over me. *We need LIBERTY through the WORD!*

2 Timothy 2:15 (KJV)

¹⁵ Study to shew thyself approved unto God, a

workman that needeth not to be ashamed, rightly dividing the word of truth. *We need to be STUDIOUS in the Word, STABLIZED in the Word, & STEADFAST in the Word!*

2 Timothy 3:16-17 (KJV)
[16] All scripture *is* given by inspiration of God, and *is* profitable for doctrine, for reproof, for correction, for instruction in righteousness: [17] That the man of God may be perfect, throughly furnished unto all good works. *We need the Word to shape our MINDS, MORALS, MISTAKES, MAINTENANCE, MODEL, MATURITY, MAKE-UP, & MINISTRY!*

- Stay Committed in Your Venture:

Proverbs 3:1-10 (KJV)
[1] My son, forget not my law; but let thine heart keep my commandments: [2] For length of days, and long life, and peace, shall they add to thee. [3] Let not mercy and truth forsake thee: bind them about thy neck; write them upon the table of thine heart: [4] So shalt thou find favour and good understanding in the sight of God and man. [5] Trust in the LORD with all thine heart; and lean not unto thine own understanding. [6] In all thy ways acknowledge him, and he shall direct thy paths. [7] Be not wise in thine own eyes: fear the LORD, and depart from evil. [8] It shall be health to thy navel, and marrow to thy bones. [9] Honour the LORD with thy substance, and with the firstfruits of all thine increase: [10] So shall thy barns be filled with plenty, and thy presses shall burst out with new wine.

- Stay Consumed With His Vision:

Matthew 4:18-20 (KJV)
[18] And Jesus, walking by the sea of Galilee, saw two

brethren, Simon called Peter, and Andrew his brother, casting a net into the sea: for they were fishers. [19] And he saith unto them, Follow me, and I will make you fishers of men. [20] And they straightway left *their* nets, and followed him.

Mark 1:14-18 (KJV)

[14] Now after that John was put in prison, Jesus came into Galilee, preaching the gospel of the kingdom of God, [15] And saying, The time is fulfilled, and the kingdom of God is at hand: repent ye, and believe the gospel. [16] Now as he walked by the sea of Galilee, he saw Simon and Andrew his brother casting a net into the sea: for they were fishers. [17] And Jesus said unto them, Come ye after me, and <u>I will make you to become fishers of men.</u> [18] And straightway they forsook their nets, and followed him.

The Scriptures are clear. The Christian life is a life of commitment.

Devotional Thoughts

_____
_____
_____
_____
_____
_____
_____
_____
_____
_____
_____
_____
_____
_____

The Great Contribution

Matthew 25:31-46 (KJV)
[31] When the Son of man shall come in his glory, and all the holy angels with him, then shall he sit upon the throne of his glory:
[32] And before him shall be gathered all nations: and he shall separate them one from another, as a shepherd divideth *his* sheep from the goats:
[33] And he shall set the sheep on his right hand, but the goats on the left.
[34] Then shall the King say unto them on his right hand, Come, ye blessed of my Father, inherit the kingdom prepared for you from the foundation of the world:
[35] For I was an hungred, and ye gave me meat: I was thirsty, and ye gave me drink: I was a stranger, and ye took me in:
[36] Naked, and ye clothed me: I was sick, and ye visited me: I was in prison, and ye came unto me.
[37] Then shall the righteous answer him, saying, Lord, when saw we thee an hungred, and fed *thee*? or thirsty, and gave *thee* drink?
[38] When saw we thee a stranger, and took *thee* in? or naked, and clothed *thee*?
[39] Or when saw we thee sick, or in prison, and came unto thee?
[40] And the King shall answer and say unto them, Verily I say unto you, Inasmuch as ye have done *it* unto one of the least of these my brethren, ye have done *it* unto me.
[41] Then shall he say also unto them on the left hand, Depart from me, ye cursed, into everlasting fire, prepared for the devil and his angels:
[42] For I was an hungred, and ye gave me no meat: I was thirsty, and ye gave me no drink:
[43] I was a stranger, and ye took me not in: naked, and ye

clothed me not: sick, and in prison, and ye visited me not. ⁴⁴ Then shall they also answer him, saying, Lord, when saw we thee an hungred, or athirst, or a stranger, or naked, or sick, or in prison, and did not minister unto thee?
⁴⁵ Then shall he answer them, saying, Verily I say unto you, Inasmuch as ye did *it* not to one of the least of these, ye did *it* not to me.
⁴⁶ And these shall go away into everlasting punishment: but the righteous into life eternal.

I think I need to say, this passage is not teaching that you must serve to be saved, but it is teaching that if you are saved you will serve. Serving, supporting, and sowing are characteristics of kingdom people.

Matthew brings us to an eschatological episode where Christ begins to share what it's going to be like when all people stand before Him to be judged. He basically says that those who have served suffers will be saved and those who have ignored peoples' pain will be punished. The passage reveals some principles that every Christian should build their lives upon, some principles that every para-church ministry should build their efforts around, some principles that every Christian organization should build their mission upon, and some principles that every church should build their ministries toward.

Devotional Thoughts

When it comes to our contribution to the kingdom........
- ❖ We Should Contribute *To Those Who Are Poor*
- ❖ We Should Contribute *To Those Who Are In Pain*
- ❖ We Should Contribute *To Those Who Are in Prison*

Let me be clear, the passage also teaches that how you treat people is the way you're treating God. Jesus what you've done for the least of these my brethren, you've done unto me and what you've not done unto the least of these, you've not done unto me. In that regard, I want you to sincerely commit to and prayerfully consider how you can bless those who are poor, those who are in pain, and those who are in prison.

Let me offer you some principles about giving to the poor.

The Principle of Restitution: *Whatever You Give To The Poor, God Gives Back To You*
> ***Proverbs 19:17 (KJV)***
> **17 He that hath pity upon the poor lendeth unto the LORD; and that which he hath given will he pay him again.**

The Principle of Reciprocity: *The Treatment That You Extend To The Poor Is The Same Treatment That Will Be Extended To You*
> ***Proverbs 21:13 (KJV)***
> **13 Whoso stoppeth his ears at the cry of the poor, he also shall cry himself, but shall not be heard.**

The Principle of Replenishment: *Those Who Are Generous Toward The Poor Are Made Prosperous by The Lord*

Proverbs 22:9 (KJV)
⁹ **He that hath a bountiful eye shall be blessed; for he giveth of his bread to the poor.**

The Principle of Righteousness: *Righteous People Are Concerned About The Poor But Rebellious People Are Cold Toward The Poor*

Proverbs 29:7 (KJV)
⁷ **The righteous considereth the cause of the poor: *but* the wicked regardeth not to know *it*.**

The Principle of Returns: *The Safest Investment That Yield The Highest Returns Is Your Investment In People*

Matthew 6:19-21 (KJV)
¹⁹ **Lay not up for yourselves treasures upon earth, where moth and rust doth corrupt, and where thieves break through and steal:**
²⁰ **But lay up for yourselves treasures in heaven, where neither moth nor rust doth corrupt, and where thieves do not break through nor steal:**
²¹ **For where your treasure is, there will your heart be also.**

Devotional Thoughts

_____
_____
_____
_____
_____
_____
_____

Christians and churches should be given to helping the hungry (when I was hungry...), helping the homeless (when I was a stranger...), helping the hard-pressed (when I was naked...), helping the hurting (when I was sick...), and helping the hemmed-in (when I was in prison...). We need ministries that empower people who are poor, ministries that encourage people who are in pain, and ministries that elevate people who are in prison. Only what you do for Christ will last and what you do for people is what you do for Christ.

The Great Commission

Matthew 28:18-20 (KJV)
[18] And Jesus came and spake unto them, saying, All power is given unto me in heaven and in earth.
[19] Go ye therefore, and teach all nations, baptizing them in the name of the Father, and of the Son, and of the Holy Ghost:
[20] Teaching them to observe all things whatsoever I have commanded you: and, lo, I am with you alway, *even* unto the end of the world. Amen.

Devotional Thoughts

_____
_____
_____
_____
_____
_____
_____
_____

These words in Matthew 28:18-20 are the Lord's last words to His disciples. Because they are His last words, they are His living will. His last words, and His living will, are to be our leading work. I believe that no matter what we do, if we're not doing The Great Commission, then we're not doing what Christ wants and wills for us to do. No matter how successful we are, if we're not successful at making disciples, then we're not successful in the eyes and estimation of Christ. Walking worthy of the Lord, be pleasing to the Lord, and being fruitful in every good work entails being disciples of Jesus Christ and building disciples of Jesus Christ.

There are several ways to teach this passage and there are great resources that have been produced that can help you grow as a disciple-making disciple. I want to offer you four things from the Great Commission passage.

> - We Must Be Given To *EVANGELISM* (because He says "go")
> - We Must Be Given To *EQUIPPING* (because He says, "teach all nations")
> - We Must Be Given To *ENLISTING* (because He says, "baptizing them")
> - We Must Be Given To *EMPOWERMENT* (because He says, "teaching them to observe"

Let me try to briefly define these terms from the text.

Evangelizing → That term go in the Greek is Poruomai, it means to carry over, to take one's self, it means to set-out. The idea is to witness as you and to go witnessing. It literally means, as you go, go for this purpose.

Equipping → That phrase "teach all nations" is better rended "make disciples of all nations" it comes from the Greek word Matheteuo, it means to learn from and become attached to one's teacher in doctrine and conduct of life. It is raising up followers of Jesus Christ who raise up followers of Jesus Christ.

Enlisting → That phrase "baptizing them" comes from the word in the Greek Baptizo, it means at least two things "Immersion & Identification." When one is baptized he/she is immersed in water in the name of Jesus Christ and is publicly identified with the redemptive work of Jesus Christ.

Empowering → The phrase "teaching them" in verse 20 comes from the word didasko in the Greek. It means to instruct by word of mouth to influence the one being taught. The thing aimed at is the shaping of the mind. You inform the mind, to impact the heart, to influence the lifestyle of those who are being taught to the glory of God.

Kingdom Christians go witnessing and witness as we go. We are ambassadors of the King, we are messengers of the King. We are witnesses of the King. We are heralds of the King. We bring Jesus to people and bring people to Jesus. Greg Laurie says, "The witnessing Christian is a happy Christian." There is no greater joy than having God use you to bring some lost person across the line of faith and seeing them place their faith in Jesus Christ for eternal salvation. Let's think about "going" for God.

- *Go Powerfully*: Mark 3:13-15; Luke 4:18-19;
- *Go Persistently*: I. Cor. 15:58
- *Go Passionately*: Mark 16:15-16
- *Go Purposefully*: Luke 19:10; John 20:21
- *Go Prolifically*: Luke 24:46-47 Acts 1:8

We Must Go Powerfully
Mark 3:13-15 (KJV)
13 And he goeth up into a mountain, and calleth *unto him* **whom he would: and they came unto him. 14 And he ordained twelve, that they should be with him, and that he might send them forth to preach, 15 And to have power to heal sicknesses, and to cast out devils:**

- *Go Under His Authority* ←(13 And he goeth up into a mountain, and calleth *unto him* whom he would: and they came unto him) **(Col. 3:16-17)**
- *Go On His Assignment* ←14 And he ordained twelve) **(John 6:38; 15:9-11)**
- *Go With His Association* ←(that they should be with him,) **(Ps.73:28; Acts 4:13; I. Cor. 1:9**

- *Go For His Agenda* ←(and that he might send them forth to preach,) **(Matthew 4:10)**
- *Go In His Ability* ←([15] And to have power to heal sicknesses, and to cast out devils) **(Acts 4:32-33; II. Cor. 1:1-5**
- *Go With His Anointing* ←*Luke 4:18-19*(**I. Cor. 4:19-20; I. Thess. 1:5)**

We Must Go Persistently
1 Corinthians 15:58 (KJV)
[58] Therefore, my beloved brethren, be ye stedfast, unmoveable, always abounding in the work of the Lord, forasmuch as ye know that your labour is not in vain in the Lord.
- *Go Constantly*← (be ye stedfast,) **Col. 1:28**
- *Go Courageously*←(unmoveable,) **II. Tim. 4:1-5**
- *Go Confidently* ←(always abounding in the work of the Lord, forasmuch as ye know that your labour is not in vain in the Lord.) **Dan. 12:3; I. Cor. 1:4-9; Josh. 1:7-9**

We Must Go Passionately
Mark 16:15-16 (KJV)
[15] And he said unto them, Go ye into all the world, and preach the gospel to every creature. [16] He that believeth and is baptized shall be saved; but he that believeth not shall be damned.
- *Be Passionate About Going* ([15] And he said unto them, Go ye into all the world) **(Luke 2;49; 4:40-43; 19:1-10; John 9:4)**
- *Be Passionate About The Good News* (and preach the gospel to every creature) **(Rom. 1:13-17I. Cor. 15:1-11; Gal. 1:1-12)**

- *Be Passionate About The Guarantee* (¹⁶ He that believeth and is baptized shall be saved; but he that believeth not shall be damned.) **(John 1:10-13; 3:16-17,36; 5:24; Rom. 10:9-13)**

We Must Go Purposefully
Luke 19:10 (KJV)
¹⁰ For the Son of man is come to seek and to save that which was lost.
John 20:21 (KJV)
²¹ Then said Jesus to them again, Peace *be* unto you: as *my* Father hath sent me, even so send I you.
- *Be About Getting People Saved* (¹⁰ For the Son of man is come to seek and to save) **(John 1:6-8; 6:25-35; 20:30-31; Rom. 10:1)**
- *Be About Getting People Sanctified* (that which was lost) **(Romans. 12:1-2; Col. 1:9-10; 2:6-7 Eph. 4:11-12)**
- *Be About Getting People Serving* (²¹ Then said Jesus to them again, Peace *be* unto you: as *my* Father hath sent me, even so send I you.) **(Eph.2:1-10)**

We Must Go Prolifically
Luke 24:46-47 (KJV)
⁴⁶ And said unto them, Thus it is written, and thus it behoved Christ to suffer, and to rise from the dead the third day:
⁴⁷ And that repentance and remission of sins should be preached in his name among all nations, beginning at Jerusalem.

_____
_____
_____

- *Proliferate His Revelation* (⁴⁶ And said unto them, Thus it is written) **Rom. 10:17**
- *Proliferate His Redemptive-Work* (and thus it behoved Christ to suffer) **(Is. 53:5-6; Col. 1:12-14)**
- *Proliferate His Resurrection* (and to rise from the dead the third day) **(Acts 2:22-24)**
- *Proliferate His Requirement* (And that repentance) **(Acts 37-41)**
- *Proliferate His Remission* (and remission of sins should be preached in his name among all nations, beginning at Jerusalem). **(Ps. 103:1-12; II. Cor. 5:21; John 2:1-2)**

Acts 1:8 (KJV)
⁸ But ye shall receive power, after that the Holy Ghost is come upon you: and ye shall be witnesses unto me both in Jerusalem, and in all Judaea, and in Samaria, and unto the uttermost part of the earth.

← Take the Gospel→
- *To Those Who Are Common*: ←*[Jerusalem]* **(Matt. 5:13-16)**
- *To Those Who Are Counter-Cultural:* ←*[all Judaea]*(**Col. 1:25-29**)
- *To The Corrupt*: ←*[Samaria]* **(Prov. 11:30; Mark 2:14-17; II. Cor. 4:1-7; James 5:19-20)**
- *To Those in Other Countries*: ←*[and unto the uttermost part of the earth]* **Matthew 24:14**

_____
_____
_____
_____
_____

In April of 1912, the largest vessel of its kind set sail in the North Atlantic Ocean. There were three messages sent to the captain and crew who were navigating the RMS Titanic. Because they ignored the messages, around 11:00 pm April 14th they hit an iceberg. It sunk the early morning of April 15, 1912. The lifeboats on which the women, children, and elite were taken to safety were only half full and the passengers did not want to return to rescue, nor wait on others while trying to save themselves. At least 1,500 people died on that cruise ship in the North Atlantic Ocean. Two tragedies, one is the leaders ignored the messages, and two, those who were safe would not do whatever possible to get others saved. As saints we must share the message and do whatever we can to get others saved or they will die and go to an abyss worse than the ocean- they will go to hell, a lake which burns with fire and brimstone. With that in mind, let's get serious about going for God.

Let's think about being disciples and building disciples. The Great-Commission Christian is a believer who is being trained and is training others to be and to do certain things. Think with me on these three things.......
   1. *Equipped & Equipping Committed People*
   2. *Equipped & Equipping Competent People &*
   3. *Equipped & Equipping Creative People*

The Duty Principle *When You Don't Live With A Great Commitment to The Great Commandment & The Great Commission, You Live A Life of Great Compromise*

Trained & Training Committed People

People Who Are Committed To The Christ

Luke 9:23-25 (KJV)
²³ And he said to *them* all, If any *man* will come after me, let him deny himself, and take up his cross daily, and follow me.
²⁴ For whosoever will save his life shall lose it: but whosoever will lose his life for my sake, the same shall save it.
²⁵ For what is a man advantaged, if he gain the whole world, and lose himself, or be cast away?

Being committed to Christ, as it is communicated from this passage implies four things.......
    1. *Seeking Christ (if any man come after me)*
    2. *Surrendering To Christ (he must first deny himself)*
    3. *Suffering For Christ (and take up his cross daily)* &
    4. *Subscribing To Christ (and follow me)*

People Who Are Committed To The Commandments

Psalm 119:9-16 (KJV)
⁹ Wherewithal shall a young man cleanse his way? by taking heed *thereto* according to thy word.
¹⁰ With my whole heart have I sought thee: O let me not wander from thy commandments.
¹¹ Thy word have I hid in mine heart, that I might not sin against thee.
¹² Blessed *art* thou, O LORD: teach me thy statutes.
¹³ With my lips have I declared all the judgments of thy mouth.

¹⁴ I have rejoiced in the way of thy testimonies, as *much as* in all riches.
¹⁵ I will meditate in thy precepts, and have respect unto thy ways.
¹⁶ I will delight myself in thy statutes: I will not forget thy word.

Commitment to the commandments means being committed to the Word of God. Commitment to the Word of God is lived out when you..........

- *Let The Word Provide Your Cleansing (v.9)*
- *Let The Word Promote Your Consecration (v.10)*
- *Let The Word Protect Your Conduct (v.11)*
- *Let The Word Provide Your Counsel (v.12)*
- *Let The Word Premise Your Conversation (v.13)*
- *Let The Word Prioritize Your Charisma (v.14)*
- *Let The Word Proliferate Your Consciousness (v.15)*
- *Let The Word Produce Your Character (v.16)*

People Who Are Committed To The Cause

Kingdom-Christians are committed to the cause of Christ. There are several ways to teach this, but to keep from being redundant, think with me on these three causes……..
    a. *The Cause of Deliverance* (Luke 15:1-24)
    b. *The Cause of Development* (II. Pet. 1:3-9)
    c. *The Cause of Deployment* (II. Tim. 3:16-17)

Christ wants to use you to

a) *Help get people delivered (Luke 4:18-19; 19:10)*
b) *Help Get People Developed (Matt. 5:17-20)*
c) *Help Get People Deployed (Matt. 9:35-38)*

Trained & Training Competent People

Kingdom Christians, disciples of Jesus Christ are competent people. They are being trained and are training others to be……..
1. **Competent to Live**
2. **Competent to Love &**
3. **Competent to Lead**

Devotional Thoughts

People Who Are Competent To Live

❖ *Stay Connected With Christ* →

John 15:1-11 (KJV)

¹ I am the true vine, and my Father is the husbandman. ² Every branch in me that beareth not fruit he taketh away: and every *branch* that beareth fruit, he purgeth it, that it may bring forth more fruit. ³ Now ye are clean through the word which I have spoken unto you. ⁴ Abide in me, and I in you. As the branch cannot bear fruit of itself, except it abide in the vine; no more can ye, except ye abide in me. ⁵ I am the vine, ye *are* the branches: He that abideth in me, and I in him, the same bringeth forth much fruit: for without me ye can do nothing. ⁶ If a man abide not in me, he is cast forth as a branch, and is withered; and men gather them, and cast *them* into the fire, and they are burned. ⁷ If ye abide in me, and my words abide in you, ye shall ask what ye will, and it shall be done unto you. ⁸ Herein is my Father glorified, that ye bear much fruit; so shall ye be my disciples. ⁹ As the Father hath loved me, so have I loved you: continue ye in my love. ¹⁰ If ye keep my commandments, ye shall abide in my love; even as I have kept my Father's commandments, and abide in his love. ¹¹ These things have I spoken unto you, that my joy might remain in you, and *that* your joy might be full.

Devotional Thoughts

_____
_____
_____
_____
_____
_____

- ❖ *Stand Through Confidence in Christ* →
Galatians 2:20 (KJV)
[20] I am crucified with Christ: nevertheless I live; yet not I, but Christ liveth in me: and the life which I now live in the flesh I live by the faith of the Son of God, who loved me, and gave himself for me.

- ❖ *Steadfastly Continue In Christ* →
Colossians 2:6-7 (KJV)
As ye have therefore received Christ Jesus the Lord, *so* walk ye in him: [7] Rooted and built up in him, and stablished in the faith, as ye have been taught, abounding therein with thanksgiving.

People Who Are Competent To Love

- <u>**They Are Consumed With God's Love**</u>

John 3:16 (KJV)
[16] For God so loved the world, that he gave his only begotten Son, that whosoever believeth in him should not perish, but have everlasting life.

Ephesians 1:4-6 (KJV)
[4] According as he hath chosen us in him before the foundation of the world, that we should be holy and without blame before him in love: [5] Having predestinated us unto the adoption of children by Jesus Christ to himself, according to the good pleasure of his will, [6] To the praise of the glory of his grace, wherein he hath made us accepted in the beloved.

- *They Are Containers of God's Love*

Matthew 22:35-37 (KJV)
35 Then one of them, *which was* a lawyer, asked *him a question*, tempting him, and saying, 36 Master, which *is* the great commandment in the law? 37 Jesus said unto him, Thou shalt love the Lord thy God with all thy heart, and with all thy soul, and with all thy mind.

Romans 5:1-5 (KJV)
1 Therefore being justified by faith, we have peace with God through our Lord Jesus Christ:
2 By whom also we have access by faith into this grace wherein we stand, and rejoice in hope of the glory of God.
3 And not only *so*, but we glory in tribulations also: knowing that tribulation worketh patience;
4 And patience, experience; and experience, hope:
5 And hope maketh not ashamed; because the love of God is shed abroad in our hearts by the Holy Ghost which is given unto us.

Romans 8:35-39 (KJV)
35 Who shall separate us from the love of Christ? *shall* tribulation, or distress, or persecution, or famine, or nakedness, or peril, or sword?
36 As it is written, For thy sake we are killed all the day long; we are accounted as sheep for the slaughter.
37 Nay, in all these things we are more than conquerors through him that loved us.
38 For I am persuaded, that neither death, nor life, nor angels, nor principalities, nor powers, nor things present, nor things to come,
39 Nor height, nor depth, nor any other creature, shall be able to separate us from the love of God, which is in Christ Jesus our Lord

- <u>*They Are Conduits of God's Love*</u>

1 John 4:7-21 (KJV)

[7] Beloved, let us love one another: for love is of God; and every one that loveth is born of God, and knoweth God. [8] He that loveth not knoweth not God; for God is love. [9] In this was manifested the love of God toward us, because that God sent his only begotten Son into the world, that we might live through him. [10] Herein is love, not that we loved God, but that he loved us, and sent his Son *to be* the propitiation for our sins. [11] Beloved, if God so loved us, we ought also to love one another. [12] No man hath seen God at any time. If we love one another, God dwelleth in us, and his love is perfected in us. [13] Hereby know we that we dwell in him, and he in us, because he hath given us of his Spirit. [14] And we have seen and do testify that the Father sent the Son *to be* the Saviour of the world. [15] Whosoever shall confess that Jesus is the Son of God, God dwelleth in him, and he in God. [16] And we have known and believed the love that God hath to us. God is love; and he that dwelleth in love dwelleth in God, and God in him. [17] Herein is our love made perfect, that we may have boldness in the day of judgment: because as he is, so are we in this world. [18] There is no fear in love; but perfect love casteth out fear: because fear hath torment. He that feareth is not made perfect in love. [19] We love him, because he first loved us. [20] If a man say, I love God, and hateth his brother, he is a liar: for he that loveth not his brother whom he hath seen, how can he love God whom he hath not seen? [21] And this commandment have we from him, That he who loveth God love his brother also.

People Who Are Competent To Lead

2 Timothy 2:1-7 (KJV)
¹ Thou therefore, my son, be strong in the grace that is in Christ Jesus. ² And the things that thou hast heard of me among many witnesses, the same commit thou to faithful men, who shall be able to teach others also. ³ Thou therefore endure hardness, as a good soldier of Jesus Christ. ⁴ No man that warreth entangleth himself with the affairs of *this* life; that he may please him who hath chosen him to be a soldier. ⁵ And if a man also strive for masteries, *yet* is he not crowned, except he strive lawfully. ⁶ The husbandman that laboureth must be first partaker of the fruits. ⁷ Consider what I say; and the Lord give thee understanding in all things.

Let's get some pointers from Paul and some help from the Holy Ghost on how to be and how to train-up some competent leaders. What follows is seven things we must learn to be and train others to be.

- *Be A Grounded Grown-up in Jesus Christ (v.1)*
- *Be A Reproducing-Reproducer for Jesus Christ (v.2)*
- *Be A Mighty Man on Mission for Jesus Christ (v.3)*
- *Be A Sold-out Soldier of Jesus Christ (v.4)*
- *Be A Disciplined Disciple of Jesus Christ (v.5)*
- *Be A Faithful Farmer for Jesus Christ (v.6)*
- *Be A Thorough Thinker in the Things of Jesus Christ (v.7)*

_____
_____
_____

The Apostle also encourages Timothy and us to (II. Timothy 2:15)
- *Be Studious (study)*
- *Be Stabilized (to shew thyself approved unto God)*
- *Be Steadfast (a workman that needeth not to be ashamed)*
- *Be Standardized(rightly dividing the word of truth)*

We must be being equipped and be being equippers. Let's be and let's build committed people, competent people, and also creative people. Think with about being trained to be and training others to be creative people.

Trained & Training Creative People

➢ We Must Be Creative In Our Walk
➢ We Must Be Creative In Our Worship
➢ We Must Be Creative In Our Works

Tom Nelson, Senior Pastor of Denton Bible Church, says that, "creativity has to do with being independently dependent upon God." The idea is that the disciple of Jesus Christ can be place in any context, any community, any crowd, any congregation, and in any country and can walk with God, worship God, and work for God successfully. They can plant churches in challenging places. They can make disciples is messy places. They can lift up God in limited places. Think with me on a few ways to be creative in the areas of our walk with God, our worship of God, and our work for God.

Being Creative In Our Walk With God

Deuteronomy 6:4-9 (KJV)

⁴ Hear, O Israel: The LORD our God *is* one LORD:
⁵ And thou shalt love the LORD thy God with all thine heart, and with all thy soul, and with all thy might.
⁶ And these words, which I command thee this day, shall be in thine heart:
⁷ And thou shalt teach them diligently unto thy children, and shalt talk of them when thou sittest in thine house, and when thou walkest by the way, and when thou liest down, and when thou risest up.
⁸ And thou shalt bind them for a sign upon thine hand, and they shall be as frontlets between thine eyes.
⁹ And thou shalt write them upon the posts of thy house, and on thy gates.

We must be creative in the since that wherever we are we let the Word govern us.
- Let The Word Govern Our Heads (v.4)
- Let The Word Govern Our Hearts (v.5-6)
- Let The Word Govern Our Homes (v.7)
- Let The Word Govern Our Hands (v.8)
- Let The Word Govern Our Habits (v.9)

Devotional Thoughts

Being Creative In Our Worship of God

Psalm 34:1-3 (KJV)
[1] I will bless the LORD at all times: his praise *shall* continually *be* in my mouth.
[2] My soul shall make her boast in the LORD: the humble shall hear *thereof*, and be glad. [3] O magnify the LORD with me, and let us exalt his name together.

Acts 16:16-34 (KJV)
[16] And it came to pass, as we went to prayer, a certain damsel possessed with a spirit of divination met us, which brought her masters much gain by soothsaying:
[17] The same followed Paul and us, and cried, saying, These men are the servants of the most high God, which shew unto us the way of salvation.
[18] And this did she many days. But Paul, being grieved, turned and said to the spirit, I command thee in the name of Jesus Christ to come out of her. And he came out the same hour.
[19] And when her masters saw that the hope of their gains was gone, they caught Paul and Silas, and drew *them* into the marketplace unto the rulers,
[20] And brought them to the magistrates, saying, These men, being Jews, do exceedingly trouble our city,
[21] And teach customs, which are not lawful for us to receive, neither to observe, being Romans.
[22] And the multitude rose up together against them: and the magistrates rent off their clothes, and commanded to beat *them*.
[23] And when they had laid many stripes upon them, they cast *them* into prison, charging the jailor to keep them safely:
[24] Who, having received such a charge, thrust them into the inner prison, and made their feet fast in the stocks.

²⁵ And at midnight Paul and Silas prayed, and sang praises unto God: and the prisoners heard them.
²⁶ And suddenly there was a great earthquake, so that the foundations of the prison were shaken: and immediately all the doors were opened, and every one's bands were loosed.
²⁷ And the keeper of the prison awaking out of his sleep, and seeing the prison doors open, he drew out his sword, and would have killed himself, supposing that the prisoners had been fled.
²⁸ But Paul cried with a loud voice, saying, Do thyself no harm: for we are all here.
²⁹ Then he called for a light, and sprang in, and came trembling, and fell down before Paul and Silas,
³⁰ And brought them out, and said, Sirs, what must I do to be saved?
³¹ And they said, Believe on the Lord Jesus Christ, and thou shalt be saved, and thy house.
³² And they spake unto him the word of the Lord, and to all that were in his house.
³³ And he took them the same hour of the night, and washed *their* stripes; and was baptized, he and all his, straightway.
³⁴ And when he had brought them into his house, he set meat before them, and rejoiced, believing in God with all his house.

Devotional Thoughts

_____
_____
_____
_____
_____
_____
_____
_____

These two passages shows how to be creative in our worship of God. It is believed that David wrote this Psalm while being pursued by enemies. It is suggested that while he was on the run, he ended up at the gates of Abimelech, the king of the Philistines. David found himself in the town of the giant Goliath whom he had killed. When God delivered him from the hand of his enemies he wrote this psalm and left us some principles about being creative in our worship of God.

- We Ought To Have A Determination To Praise God (I will bless the Lord)
- We Ought To Be Diligent in Our Praise of God (I will bless the Lords at all times)
- We Ought To Offer Declarative Praise to God (his praise shall continually be in my mouth)
- We Ought To Have A Demonstrative Praise of God (the humble shall hear thereof and be glad)
- We Ought To Have A Disposition of Praise Toward God (O, Magnify the Lord with me, and let us exalt his name together)

You can be determined to praise/worship God in any and all circumstances. You can diligently praise/worship God by keeping your mind stayed on Him. You can make sure that you're not just praising, but also worshiping by not just celebrating what He has done, but also by acknowledging and declaring who He is. You can creatively demonstrate to others what it looks like to praise God without restraints and limitations. You can model a disposition of praise/worship when you see God as sovereign and see His name above all other names.

Paul and Silas were place in a dark, damp, and deep dungeon. They were imprisoned because Paul had cast out a demon, which had possessed a damsel. They didn't complain and they didn't crumble. They worshiped God. Their praise and worship reveals four principles about worship and being creative in our worship.

1. True Worship Cannot Be Confined
2. True Worship Cannot Be Constricted
3. True Worship Cannot be Contained &
4. True Worship is not Conditional

Be a true worshiper. Paul often praised God in prison. His praise and worship was not confined. When Peter was arrested for preaching the Gospel, he praise God for suffering for His name. His worship was not constricted. Jeremiah had said he would not speak on God's behalf anymore, but it was like fire shut up in his bones. His worship couldn't be contained. Paul, Peter, Jeremiah, and David praised God under pressure, they praised God in unfavorable predicaments, and they praised God while facing overwhelming problems. In other words, their worship was not conditional. Be a true worshiper. As it relates to creativity in your worship, you don't need things to be going well. You don't need favorable circumstances. You don't need the right instruments and music. You don't need a praise-team, a choir, or an orchestra. What you need is a heart that is bent toward God and humbled toward God.

Being Creative In Our Work For God

I talked earlier about the power of partnership and about how teamwork makes the dream work. I used the passage from Mark 2:1-12. In that passage there are some principles to learned about being creative in our work for God. Since you can't ever read too much Bible, let me place the passage before you again.

Mark 2:1-12 (KJV)
[1] And again he entered into Capernaum after *some* days; and it was noised that he was in the house. [2] And straightway many were gathered together, insomuch that there was no room to receive *them*, no, not so much as about the door: and he preached the word unto them. [3] And they come unto him, bringing one sick of the palsy, which was borne of four. [4] And when they could not come nigh unto him for the press, they uncovered the roof where he was: and when they had broken *it* up, they let down the bed wherein the sick of the palsy lay. [5] When Jesus saw their faith, he said unto the sick of the palsy, Son, thy sins be forgiven thee. [6] But there were certain of the scribes sitting there, and reasoning in their hearts, [7] Why doth this *man* thus speak blasphemies? who can forgive sins but God only? [8] And immediately when Jesus perceived in his spirit that they so reasoned within themselves, he said unto them, Why reason ye these things in your hearts? [9] Whether is it easier to say to the sick of the palsy, *Thy* sins be forgiven thee; or to say, Arise, and take up thy bed, and walk? [10] But that ye may know that the Son of man hath power on earth to forgive sins, (he saith to the sick of the palsy,) [11] I say unto thee, Arise, and take up thy bed, and go

thy way into thine house. ¹² And immediately he arose, took up the bed, and went forth before them all; insomuch that they were all amazed, and glorified God, saying, We never saw it on this fashion.

In the text there were some problems that kept the four men from getting the one paralytic man to Jesus. There was the problem of human limitations. One, two, nor three could lift the bed with the man on it. Therefore they couldn't get him to Jesus. There was the problem of people being in the way that hindered the four from getting the one to Jesus. And, there was the problem of structure. The building was not conducive to getting the man to Jesus. I just want to offer three principles that will help us be creative in our work for God.

The Principle of Redemptive Partnerships
Sometimes a job is too big, a task is too challenging, and a goal is lofty for us to reach alone. We must involve other likeminded people.

Ecclesiastes 4:9-12 (KJV)
⁹ Two *are* better than one; because they have a good reward for their labour.
¹⁰ For if they fall, the one will lift up his fellow: but woe to him *that is* alone when he falleth; for *he hath* not another to help him up.
¹¹ Again, if two lie together, then they have heat: but how can one be warm *alone*?
¹² And if one prevail against him, two shall withstand him; and a threefold cord is not quickly broken.

The Principle of Restructuring Programs & Places
Sometimes you have to change the structure of places and programs to reach certain people. The old way of doing things, and the old venue of getting people in, does more to hinder the mission than to help the mission.

Matthew 9:14-17 (KJV)
[14] Then came to him the disciples of John, saying, Why do we and the Pharisees fast oft, but thy disciples fast not?
[15] And Jesus said unto them, Can the children of the bridechamber mourn, as long as the bridegroom is with them? but the days will come, when the bridegroom shall be taken from them, and then shall they fast.
[16] No man putteth a piece of new cloth unto an old garment, for that which is put in to fill it up taketh from the garment, and the rent is made worse.
[17] Neither do men put new wine into old bottles: else the bottles break, and the wine runneth out, and the bottles perish: but they put new wine into new bottles, and both are preserved.

The Principle of Routing Around Problem People
Sometimes you must move beyond and without those who get in the way of accomplishing the mission.

Mark 5:35-43 (KJV)
[35] While he yet spake, there came from the ruler of the synagogue's *house certain* which said, Thy daughter is dead: why troublest thou the Master any further?
[36] As soon as Jesus heard the word that was spoken, he saith unto the ruler of the synagogue, Be not afraid, only believe.
[37] And he suffered no man to follow him, save Peter, and James, and John the brother of James.
[38] And he cometh to the house of the ruler of the

synagogue, and seeth the tumult, and them that wept and wailed greatly.

³⁹ And when he was come in, he saith unto them, Why make ye this ado, and weep? the damsel is not dead, but sleepeth.

⁴⁰ And they laughed him to scorn. But when he had put them all out, he taketh the father and the mother of the damsel, and them that were with him, and entereth in where the damsel was lying.

⁴¹ And he took the damsel by the hand, and said unto her, Talitha cumi; which is, being interpreted, Damsel, I say unto thee, arise.

⁴² And straightway the damsel arose, and walked; for she was *of the age* of twelve years. And they were astonished with a great astonishment.

⁴³ And he charged them straitly that no man should know it; and commanded that something should be given her to eat.

Devotional Thoughts

The Great Commission also calls for Enlistment & Empowerment. When Jesus said, baptizing them in the name of the Father, and of the Son, and of the Holy Ghost," He was commanding two things, immersion and identification. The term for baptizing, "baptizo" means to fully immerse. It also means to fully identify. My Pastor teaches that going into the water represents the death of Christ, going under the water represents the burial of Christ, and coming out of the water represents the resurrection of Christ. In the New Testament Paul used the phrase, "baptized unto Moses." In I. Corinthians 10:1-12, he was referring to the fact that those Israelites who followed Moses across the Red Sea were identified with Moses. When a new believer connects with a local church, that new believer is identifying with Christ through faith, through family and through fellowship. As my pastor says, "if it's right to be in church, then it's wrong to be out of church." Dr. Adrian Rogers once said, "Show me a person that does not love the local church, and I will show you a person who does not love Jesus." You can follow Jesus and not fellowship with His people.

Hebrews 10:24-25 (KJV)
24 And let us consider one another to provoke unto love and to good works:
25 Not forsaking the assembling of ourselves together, as the manner of some *is;* **but exhorting** *one another:* **and so much the more, as ye see the day approaching.**

_____
_____
_____
_____

Empowering, as I'm using the term, means to inform, to instruct, and to impact people through the Word of God. Jesus said literally, teaching them to obey." We must impart the Word to impact people's walk.

1 Timothy 4:6-16 (KJV)
⁶ If thou put the brethren in remembrance of these things, thou shalt be a good minister of Jesus Christ, nourished up in the words of faith and of good doctrine, whereunto thou hast attained.
⁷ But refuse profane and old wives' fables, and exercise thyself *rather* unto godliness.
⁸ For bodily exercise profiteth little: but godliness is profitable unto all things, having promise of the life that now is, and of that which is to come.
⁹ This *is* a faithful saying and worthy of all acceptation.
¹⁰ For therefore we both labour and suffer reproach, because we trust in the living God, who is the Saviour of all men, specially of those that believe.
¹¹ These things command and teach.
¹² Let no man despise thy youth; but be thou an example of the believers, in word, in conversation, in charity, in spirit, in faith, in purity.
¹³ Till I come, give attendance to reading, to exhortation, to doctrine.
¹⁴ Neglect not the gift that is in thee, which was given thee by prophecy, with the laying on of the hands of the presbytery.
¹⁵ Meditate upon these things; give thyself wholly to them; that thy profiting may appear to all.
¹⁶ Take heed unto thyself, and unto the doctrine; continue in them: for in doing this thou shalt both save thyself, and them that hear thee.

_____
_____

2 Timothy 3:16-4:5 (KJV)
[16] All scripture *is* given by inspiration of God, and *is* profitable for doctrine, for reproof, for correction, for instruction in righteousness:
[17] That the man of God may be perfect, throughly furnished unto all good works.
[1] I charge *thee* therefore before God, and the Lord Jesus Christ, who shall judge the quick and the dead at his appearing and his kingdom;
[2] Preach the word; be instant in season, out of season; reprove, rebuke, exhort with all longsuffering and doctrine.
[3] For the time will come when they will not endure sound doctrine; but after their own lusts shall they heap to themselves teachers, having itching ears;
[4] And they shall turn away *their* ears from the truth, and shall be turned unto fables.
[5] But watch thou in all things, endure afflictions, do the work of an evangelist, make full proof of thy ministry.

- Teach for *Sanctification* (Col. 3:16-17)
- Teach for *Transformation* (Romans 12:1-2)
- Teach for *Reorientation* (Col. 3:10)
- Teach for *Multiplication* (II. Tim. 2:2)

I'm praying that you grow in the likeness of Jesus Christ. I'm praying that you be fruitful in the work of evangelizing, of equipping, of enlisting, and of empowering.

I pray that you be a great Christian, a Great Commandment Christian, a Great Companionship Christian, a Great Commitment Christian, a Great Contribution Christian, and a Great Commission Christian.

Chapter Eight
Be Furthered In Our Witness of God

"and increasing in the knowledge of God"

The Dynamic Principle *Growth Inside Fuels Growth Outside*

The Principle of KNOWING GOD
The more you know about God and the more you know God, the better equipped you are to be a witness for God.

1 John 1:1-4 (KJV)
¹ That which was from the beginning, which we have heard, which we have seen with our eyes, which we have looked upon, and our hands have handled, of the Word of life;
² (For the life was manifested, and we have seen *it*, and bear witness, and shew unto you that eternal life, which was with the Father, and was manifested unto us;)
³ That which we have seen and heard declare we unto you, that ye also may have fellowship with us: and truly our fellowship *is* with the Father, and with his Son Jesus Christ.
⁴ And these things write we unto you, that your joy may be full.

Devotional Thoughts

_____
_____
_____
_____

The Principle of SHOWING-OFF GOD
The more you know Christ, the more you can show Christ to others.

You can be an extension of His presence, an expression of His Person, an example of His passion, and an exhibition of His power.

Acts 4:13 (KJV)
13 Now when they saw the boldness of Peter and John, and perceived that they were unlearned and ignorant men, they marvelled; and they took knowledge of them, that they had been with Jesus.

The Principle of GROWING IN GOD
The more you know, the more you grow.

2 Peter 1:3-8 (KJV)
3 According as his divine power hath given unto us all things that *pertain* unto life and godliness, through the knowledge of him that hath called us to glory and virtue:
4 Whereby are given unto us exceeding great and precious promises: that by these ye might be partakers of the divine nature, having escaped the corruption that is in the world through lust.
5 And beside this, giving all diligence, add to your faith virtue; and to virtue knowledge;
6 And to knowledge temperance; and to temperance patience; and to patience godliness;
7 And to godliness brotherly kindness; and to brotherly kindness charity.
8 For if these things be in you, and abound, they make *you that ye shall* neither *be* barren nor unfruitful in the knowledge of our Lord Jesus Christ.

The Principle of FLOWING IN GOD

As you grow in grace, you also grow in the operation of the gifts God has given you.

2 Timothy 2:20-26 (KJV)
[20] But in a great house there are not only vessels of gold and of silver, but also of wood and of earth; and some to honour, and some to dishonour.
[21] If a man therefore purge himself from these, he shall be a vessel unto honour, sanctified, and meet for the master's use, *and* prepared unto every good work.
[22] Flee also youthful lusts: but follow righteousness, faith, charity, peace, with them that call on the Lord out of a pure heart.
[23] But foolish and unlearned questions avoid, knowing that they do gender strifes.
[24] And the servant of the Lord must not strive; but be gentle unto all *men*, apt to teach, patient,
[25] In meekness instructing those that oppose themselves; if God peradventure will give them repentance to the acknowledging of the truth;
[26] And *that* they may recover themselves out of the snare of the devil, who are taken captive by him at his will.

Devotional Thoughts

The Principle of SOWING FOR GOD

The more you know, the more you grow, and the more you know, the more you sow.

When it comes to sowing and reaping, we must remember that we reap what we sow. If you sow watermelons, you don't get tomatoes, you get water melons. If you sow that which is good, you get that which is good. If you sow time in devotion, you reap times of devotedness. If you sow time in development, you reap times of development. You get the picture. When you sow into God's kingdom, you reap the blessings of God's kingdom.

Matthew 25:14-30 (KJV)
[14] For *the kingdom of heaven is* as a man travelling into a far country, *who* called his own servants, and delivered unto them his goods.
[15] And unto one he gave five talents, to another two, and to another one; to every man according to his several ability; and straightway took his journey.
[16] Then he that had received the five talents went and traded with the same, and made *them* other five talents.
[17] And likewise he that *had received* two, he also gained other two.
[18] But he that had received one went and digged in the earth, and hid his lord's money.
[19] After a long time the lord of those servants cometh, and reckoneth with them.
[20] And so he that had received five talents came and brought other five talents, saying, Lord, thou deliveredst unto me five talents: behold, I have gained beside them five talents more.
[21] His lord said unto him, Well done, *thou* good and

faithful servant: thou hast been faithful over a few things, I will make thee ruler over many things: enter thou into the joy of thy lord.

²² He also that had received two talents came and said, Lord, thou deliveredst unto me two talents: behold, I have gained two other talents beside them.

²³ His lord said unto him, Well done, good and faithful servant; thou hast been faithful over a few things, I will make thee ruler over many things: enter thou into the joy of thy lord.

²⁴ Then he which had received the one talent came and said, Lord, I knew thee that thou art an hard man, reaping where thou hast not sown, and gathering where thou hast not strawed:

²⁵ And I was afraid, and went and hid thy talent in the earth: lo, *there* thou hast *that is* thine.

²⁶ His lord answered and said unto him, *Thou* wicked and slothful servant, thou knewest that I reap where I sowed not, and gather where I have not strawed:

²⁷ Thou oughtest therefore to have put my money to the exchangers, and *then* at my coming I should have received mine own with usury.

²⁸ Take therefore the talent from him, and give *it* unto him which hath ten talents.

²⁹ For unto every one that hath shall be given, and he shall have abundance: but from him that hath not shall be taken away even that which he hath.

³⁰ And cast ye the unprofitable servant into outer darkness: there shall be weeping and gnashing of teeth.

Devotional Thoughts

_____
_____
_____
_____
_____

The Principle of GOING FOR GOD

The more you grow, the more you witness and the more you witness, the more you grow.

Acts 1:8 (KJV)
⁸ But ye shall receive power, after that the Holy Ghost is come upon you: and ye shall be witnesses unto me both in Jerusalem, and in all Judaea, and in Samaria, and unto the uttermost part of the earth.

The early Church expanded in their witness as they expanded in their walk. Their geographical expansion came alongside their theological expansion. As they came to know Christ more, they help to help more people know Christ. The same is true for us. Let's be furthered in our witness. Let's increase in knowing, in growing, in show, in flowing, in sowing, and in going.

Devotional Thoughts

_____
_____
_____
_____
_____
_____
_____
_____
_____
_____
_____
_____

Chapter Nine
Be Fortified For Warfare Through God

"strengthened with all might according to his glorious power"

The apostle uses the phrase "strengthened with all might according to his glorious power." That phrase in the Greek actually means receiving ability and capability from an outside power-source. I love to hear my Pastor tell the story of a blackout in New York. He says that one year there was a statewide blackout and no lights shined in New York except the lights in Lady Liberty. While everything, every building, every house, and every street was black dark, lady Liberty still shined brightly. Well, once they got the problem fixed they set out to discover why the Statue of Liberty beamed brightly while everything and every other place was dark. What they found was that the Statue of Liberty was connected to a power-source in Pennsylvania. She was powered by a source outside of herself. Wow. That's what we need. We need to be connected to a Source outside of ourselves. That source is Jesus Christ. That Source is the wonderful Holy Spirit. That Source is not just God with us, God over us, and God for us, but that Source is God in us! In my previous book: The Blessed Life, I share twelve steps to victory from Ephesians 6:10-18. In that book I explain that we must maintain a connection with Christ in order to defeat the devil. In this book I just want to offer four principles.

The Association Principle
You are not fit for warfare if you are not fellowshipping in worship.

Joshua 3:5 (KJV)
⁵ And Joshua said unto the people, Sanctify yourselves: for to morrow the LORD will do wonders among you.

Ephesians 6:10 (KJV)
¹⁰ Finally, my brethren, be strong in the Lord, and in the power of his might.

The Armor Principle
You cannot fully contend for God if you are not fully covered with God.

Ephesians 6:11 (KJV)
¹¹ Put on the whole armour of God, that ye may be able to stand against the wiles of the devil.

Devotional Thoughts

_____
_____
_____
_____
_____
_____
_____
_____
_____
_____
_____
_____

The Ambassador Principle

Your representation determines your refuge. God is a refuge only to those who represent Him.

2 Corinthians 5:17-20 (KJV)
[17] Therefore if any man be in Christ, he is a new creature: old things are passed away; behold, all things are become new.
[18] And all things are of God, who hath reconciled us to himself by Jesus Christ, and hath given to us the ministry of reconciliation;
[19] To wit, that God was in Christ, reconciling the world unto himself, not imputing their trespasses unto them; and hath committed unto us the word of reconciliation.
[20] Now then we are ambassadors for Christ, as though God did beseech you by us: we pray you in Christ's stead, be ye reconciled to God.

2 Corinthians 10:3-5 (KJV)
[3] For though we walk in the flesh, we do not war after the flesh:
[4] (For the weapons of our warfare *are* not carnal, but mighty through God to the pulling down of strong holds;)
[5] Casting down imaginations, and every high thing that exalteth itself against the knowledge of God, and bringing into captivity every thought to the obedience of Christ;

Psalm 46:1-11 (KJV)
[1] God *is* our refuge and strength, a very present help in trouble.

² Therefore will not we fear, though the earth be removed, and though the mountains be carried into the midst of the sea;
³ *Though* the waters thereof roar *and* be troubled, *though* the mountains shake with the swelling thereof. Selah.
⁴ *There is* a river, the streams whereof shall make glad the city of God, the holy *place* of the tabernacles of the most High.
⁵ God *is* in the midst of her; she shall not be moved: God shall help her, *and that* right early.
⁶ The heathen raged, the kingdoms were moved: he uttered his voice, the earth melted.
⁷ The LORD of hosts *is* with us; the God of Jacob *is* our refuge. Selah.
⁸ Come, behold the works of the LORD, what desolations he hath made in the earth.
⁹ He maketh wars to cease unto the end of the earth; he breaketh the bow, and cutteth the spear in sunder; he burneth the chariot in the fire.
¹⁰ Be still, and know that I *am* God: I will be exalted among the heathen, I will be exalted in the earth.
¹¹ The LORD of hosts *is* with us; the God of Jacob *is* our refuge. Selah.

The Army Principle

You cannot be successful at warfare if you are succumbed by the world.

2 Timothy 2:3-4 (KJV)
³ Thou therefore endure hardness, as a good soldier of Jesus Christ.
⁴ No man that warreth entangleth himself with the affairs of *this* life; that he may please him who hath chosen him to be a soldier.

I love Colossians 1:11. The passage says that we can be strengthened with God's strength. We can be powered by God's power. We can receive so much strength from God that we have patience and longsuffering with joyfulness. This is huge. The term patience comes from the Greek word *hupomeno*, which means to bear under hard predicaments. The term longsuffering comes from the Greek word *makrothumeo*, which means to bear under hard people. The verse is teaching that we can get so strengthened and so powered by God that we can bear under hard predicaments and hard people and still have joy.

I pray that you be fortified by God. I pray that you be a strong soldier of Jesus Christ. I pray that you walk under the covering of God. I pray that yoou be victorious in spiritual warfare.

Devotional Thoughts

Chapter Ten
Be Festive In Our Worship of God

"Giving Thanks Unto The Father"

The Apostle Paul encourages the readers to praise God. Praise becomes the believer. We talked about praise and worship earlier in the book but I just want to pull from this passage seven things you should praise God for.

Praise Him for your *Relationship* = "Father"

The text says, "Giving thanks unto the Father." The only way to correctly or rightfully address God as Father is to have a relationship with Him. Did you know, having a relationship with God is the greatest blessing you can receive and the greatest invitation you can extend.

John 1:10-13 (KJV)
[10] He was in the world, and the world was made by him, and the world knew him not.
[11] He came unto his own, and his own received him not.
[12] But as many as received him, to them gave he power to become the sons of God, *even* to them that believe on his name:
[13] Which were born, not of blood, nor of the will of the flesh, nor of the will of man, but of God.

Romans 8:14-16 (KJV)
14 For as many as are led by the Spirit of God, they are the sons of God.
15 For ye have not received the spirit of bondage again to fear; but ye have received the Spirit of adoption, whereby we cry, Abba, Father.
16 The Spirit itself beareth witness with our spirit, that we are the children of God:

1 John 3:1-2 (KJV)
1 Behold, what manner of love the Father hath bestowed upon us, that we should be called the sons of God: therefore the world knoweth us not, because it knew him not.
2 Beloved, now are we the sons of God, and it doth not yet appear what we shall be: but we know that, when he shall appear, we shall be like him; for we shall see him as he is.

Philippians 2:12-15 (KJV)
12 Wherefore, my beloved, as ye have always obeyed, not as in my presence only, but now much more in my absence, work out your own salvation with fear and trembling.
13 For it is God which worketh in you both to will and to do of *his* good pleasure.
14 Do all things without murmurings and disputings:
15 That ye may be blameless and harmless, the sons of God, without rebuke, in the midst of a crooked and perverse nation, among whom ye shine as lights in the world;

> Praise Him for your *Regeneration* = "made us meet"

The text says, "which hath made us meet." God has groomed us for glory. He has fitted us for an eternal future. God has prepared us for paradise. God has honed us for heaven. Nothing in us qualified us for a relationship with Him on earth, nor a residence with Him in eternity. God did it. We should praise God for making us hellish mortals into heavenly material.

Ephesians 1:13-14 (KJV)
13 In whom ye also *trusted*, after that ye heard the word of truth, the gospel of your salvation: in whom also after that ye believed, ye were sealed with that holy Spirit of promise,
14 Which is the earnest of our inheritance until the redemption of the purchased possession, unto the praise of his glory.

Devotional Thoughts

> Praise Him for your *Release*= "delivered us from the power of darkness"

The text says, "who hath delivered us from the power of darkness." It makes me think about that old Negro spiritual that says, "I'm so glad that Jesus lifted me." We were bound by Satan, we were bound by sin, and we were bound by selfishness, but God broke all those bonds and delivered us from the power of darkness. We shouldn't take for granted the fact that, if the Lord hadn't released us, Satan would have ravished us. We ought to lift Him up for liberating us.

Psalm 107:2 (KJV)
[2] Let the redeemed of the LORD say *so*, whom he hath redeemed from the hand of the enemy;

Luke 4:18-19 (KJV)
[18] The Spirit of the Lord *is* upon me, because he hath anointed me to preach the gospel to the poor; he hath sent me to heal the brokenhearted, to preach deliverance to the captives, and recovering of sight to the blind, to set at liberty them that are bruised,
[19] To preach the acceptable year of the Lord.

2 Corinthians 3:17 (KJV)
[17] Now the Lord is that Spirit: and where the Spirit of the Lord *is*, there *is* liberty.

Hebrews 2:14-15 (KJV)
[14] Forasmuch then as the children are partakers of flesh and blood, he also himself likewise took part of the same; that through death he might destroy him

that had the power of death, that is, the devil;
¹⁵ And deliver them who through fear of death were all their lifetime subject to bondage.

> Praise Him for your *Relocation* = "translated us into the kingdom"

The text says that he has, "translated us into the kingdom of his dear Son." God has placed us in the body of Christ. God has moved us out of the jurisdiction of the devil, and into the jurisdiction of our Deliverer. God relocated us from the reign and residence of Satan, to the reign and residence of His Son. We no longer live under the dictatorship of Satan, we now walk in the deliverance of our Savior. We are kingdom people because of our kingdom placement. We have kingdom privileges, kingdom prowess, Kingdom protection, kingdom provisions, and kingdom promises because of our kingdom placement. Praise God for your relocation.

Ephesians 1:1-7 (KJV)
¹ **Paul, an apostle of Jesus Christ by the will of God, to the saints which are at Ephesus, and to the faithful in Christ Jesus:**
² **Grace** *be* **to you, and peace, from God our Father, and** *from* **the Lord Jesus Christ.**
³ **Blessed** *be* **the God and Father of our Lord Jesus Christ, who hath blessed us with all spiritual blessings in heavenly** *places* **in Christ:**
⁴ **According as he hath chosen us in him before the foundation of the world, that we should be holy and without blame before him in love:**

⁵ Having predestinated us unto the adoption of children by Jesus Christ to himself, according to the good pleasure of his will,
⁶ To the praise of the glory of his grace, wherein he hath made us accepted in the beloved.
⁷ In whom we have redemption through his blood, the forgiveness of sins, according to the riches of his grace;

Praise Him for your *Redemption* = "we have redemption"

The text teaches that we have redemption in Christ. The word redemption comes from *apolutrosis* in the Greek. It means to buy out of captivity. Sin was the captivity, the sinner is the captive, and the life of Jesus was the cost for the sinner's release. The picture is that of a slave who was up for sale to other slave-owners. However, the person who bought the slave bought him and set the slave free. I love the chorus to Ms. Elvina Hall's hymn, "Jesus paid it all, all to him I owe. Sin had left a crimson stain –He washed it white as snow." Praise God for offering His only begotten Son to Himself as the only sufficient sacrifice for your sins.

Isaiah 53:5-6 (KJV)
⁵ But he *was* wounded for our transgressions, *he was* bruised for our iniquities: the chastisement of our peace *was* upon him; and with his stripes we are healed.
⁶ All we like sheep have gone astray; we have turned every one to his own way; and the LORD hath laid on him the iniquity of us all.

> Praise Him for your *Ratification* = "through his blood"

The text teaches that the redemption came through His blood. This is a reference to the full atoning work of Christ. Jesus gave himself through His life and He gave himself through His death. His life was a satisfying and sufficient sacrifice and His death was a satisfying and sufficient sacrifice. His life and death was satisfying and sufficient enough to turn away the wrath of God and expiate the guilt of man. We ought to praise God for Jesus and praise Jesus for doing for us what we could never do for ourselves.

Romans 3:23-26 (KJV)
[23] For all have sinned, and come short of the glory of God;
[24] Being justified freely by his grace through the redemption that is in Christ Jesus:
[25] Whom God hath set forth *to be* a propitiation through faith in his blood, to declare his righteousness for the remission of sins that are past, through the forbearance of God;
[26] To declare, *I say*, at this time his righteousness: that he might be just, and the justifier of him which believeth in Jesus.

1 John 2:1-2 (KJV)
[1] My little children, these things write I unto you, that ye sin not. And if any man sin, we have an advocate with the Father, Jesus Christ the righteous:
[2] And he is the propitiation for our sins: and not for ours only, but also for *the sins of* the whole world

> Praise Him for your *Record* = "even the forgiveness of sin"

This passage and many others declare that we are forgiven. Our slate is clean. We have a new record. I celebrate that my past, my present, and my future sin is eternally forgiven. Forgiveness gives us a future. Forgiveness gives us fresh-starts. Forgiveness gives us a right to keep going, keep growing, keep flowing, and keep sowing. These things are true, not just in our relationship with God, but also in our relationships with other people. Praise God for your record!

Psalm 103:3 (KJV)
³ Who forgiveth all thine iniquities; who healeth all thy diseases;

Psalm 103:10 (KJV)
¹⁰ He hath not dealt with us after our sins; nor rewarded us according to our iniquities.

Psalm 103:12 (KJV)
¹² As far as the east is from the west, *so* far hath he removed our transgressions from us.

> **God forgives us...........**
> Of Our *Sin (that's innate)*
>
> *Of Our Sins (that's involvement)*
>
> *Of Our Sinfulness (that's iniquity)*

Praise God For Forgiveness of Your Sin
The Innate

Psalm 51:5 (KJV)
5 Behold, I was shapen in iniquity; and in sin did my mother conceive me.

Romans 5:12 (KJV)
12 Wherefore, as by one man sin entered into the world, and death by sin; and so death passed upon all men, for that all have sinned:

Praise God For Forgiveness of Your Sins
The Involvement

1 John 1:9 (KJV)
9 If we confess our sins, he is faithful and just to forgive us *our* sins, and to cleanse us from all unrighteousness.

Praise God For Forgiveness of Your Sinfulness
The Iniquity

Psalm 51:1-2 (KJV)
1 Have mercy upon me, O God, according to thy lovingkindness: according unto the multitude of thy tender mercies blot out my transgressions.
2 Wash me throughly from mine iniquity, and cleanse me from my sin.

Psalm 119:133 (KJV)
133 Order my steps in thy word: and let not any iniquity have dominion over me.

Implies A *Freeing* (Ps. 103:3a)
Romans 8:1-2 (KJV)
¹ *There is* therefore now no condemnation to them which are in Christ Jesus, who walk not after the flesh, but after the Spirit.
² For the law of the Spirit of life in Christ Jesus hath made me free from the law of sin and death.

John 8:31-36 (KJV)
³¹ Then said Jesus to those Jews which believed on him, If ye continue in my word, *then* are ye my disciples indeed;
³² And ye shall know the truth, and the truth shall make you free.
³³ They answered him, We be Abraham's seed, and were never in bondage to any man: how sayest thou, Ye shall be made free?
³⁴ Jesus answered them, Verily, verily, I say unto you, Whosoever committeth sin is the servant of sin.
³⁵ And the servant abideth not in the house for ever: *but* the Son abideth ever.
³⁶ If the Son therefore shall make you free, ye shall be free indeed.

When you walk in the awareness and assurance of God's forgiveness you can worship with liberty and pray without shame.

When you come to know how the Bible explains forgiveness you can move from being sabotaged by guild and serve the living God. Guilt will paralyze and immobilize you, but forgiveness frees and fixes you.

Implies A *Fixing-Up* (Ps. 103:3b-4)
Hebrews 9:13-14 (KJV)
¹³ For if the blood of bulls and of goats, and the ashes of an heifer sprinkling the unclean, sanctifieth to the purifying of the flesh:
¹⁴ How much more shall the blood of Christ, who through the eternal Spirit offered himself without spot to God, purge your conscience from dead works to serve the living God?

Implies A *Forgetting* (Ps. 103:7-8)
Hebrews 8:10-12 (KJV)
¹⁰ For this *is* the covenant that I will make with the house of Israel after those days, saith the Lord; I will put my laws into their mind, and write them in their hearts: and I will be to them a God, and they shall be to me a people:
¹¹ And they shall not teach every man his neighbour, and every man his brother, saying, Know the Lord: for all shall know me, from the least to the greatest.
¹² For I will be merciful to their unrighteousness, and their sins and their iniquities will I remember no more.

Micah 7:18-19 (KJV)
¹⁸ Who *is* a God like unto thee, that pardoneth iniquity, and passeth by the transgression of the remnant of his heritage? he retaineth not his anger for ever, because he delighteth *in* mercy.
¹⁹ He will turn again, he will have compassion upon us; he will subdue our iniquities; and thou wilt cast all their sins into the depths of the sea.

Job 14:17 (KJV)
¹⁷ My transgression *is* sealed up in a bag, and thou sewest up mine iniquity.

I certainly don't want to imply that you have a license to sin, but I do want you to know that you can be liberated from self-imposed guilt over your sins. Don't let your past failures keep you from growing in your fellowship with and faithfulness to God.

Implies A *Future:* (Ps. 103:10-14)
Romans 8:14-18 (KJV)
¹⁴ For as many as are led by the Spirit of God, they are the sons of God.
¹⁵ For ye have not received the spirit of bondage again to fear; but ye have received the Spirit of adoption, whereby we cry, Abba, Father.
¹⁶ The Spirit itself beareth witness with our spirit, that we are the children of God:
¹⁷ And if children, then heirs; heirs of God, and joint-heirs with Christ; if so be that we suffer with *him*, that we may be also glorified together.
¹⁸ For I reckon that the sufferings of this present time *are* not worthy *to be compared* with the glory which shall be revealed in us.

We can boldly march into the throne-room of grace because we're forgiven. We can be delivered from depression and released from regrets because we are forgiven. We can get up out of our sin, get over the pain of our sins, and try to please God again because we're forgiven. Praise God for your record!

> *Praise the Lord because............*
> *•You Live Through A New Reality (v.12 -God is now your Father)*
> *•You Live Under A New Ruler (v.13a -God has delivered you from the devil)*
> *•You Live In A New Realm (v.13b -God has placed you in the kingdom of Jesus Christ)*
> *•You Live With A New Record (v.14 -God has eternally erased the record of your sins)*

You Live Through A New Reality (v.12)
  Remember the Reality of
      -Your Father: {the Father} (Romans 8:14-15)
      -Your Fortunes: {the inheritance} (Romans 8:16-17; Ephesians 1:13-14)
      -Your Family: {the saints} (Ephesians 2:19-22)
      -Your Future: {in light} (Romans 8:18; Col. 1:27; I. Peter 1:3-9; I. John 3:1-2)

You Live Under A New Ruler (v.13)
  Revel in the Reality that (Ephesians 2:1-10)
      You Were Dead In Sin: 2:1
      You Were Directed By Satan: 2:2
      You Were Dominated By Selfishness: 2:3
      You Have Been Delivered By The Sovereign: 2:4-5
      You Are Dwelling In The Savior: 2:6
      You Are Designed For His Service: 2:7-10

You Live In A New Realm (v.13b)
  Respond to the Reality that
      You Reside In Christ (I. Cor. 5:17; Col. 1:27)
      You Are The Residence of Christ (Rom. 8:1; 8:8-11; Col. 1:28)
      You Are Royalty Through Christ (I. Pet. 2:9)

You Live With A New Record (v.14)

Receive the Reality of
>Your Salvation (John 3:16-17)
>Your Sanctification (Romans 5:17-21)
>Your Justification (Romans 5:1)

Praise God for your new reality, for your new Ruler, for your new realm, and for your new record.

I hope these principles and pointers have been a blessing to you. I pray that you be filled with the Word of God, that you be faithful in your walk with God, that you be focused on the will of God, that you be fruitful in the work of God, that you be furthered in your witness of God, that you be fortified for warfare through God, and that you be festive in your worship of God.

Devotional Thoughts

Section Three

Principles from the Apostle's Proclamation

Colossians 1:12-21 (KJV)

¹² Giving thanks unto the Father, which hath made us meet to be partakers of the inheritance of the saints in light: ¹³ Who hath delivered us from the power of darkness, and hath translated *us* into the kingdom of his dear Son: ¹⁴ In whom we have redemption through his blood, *even* the forgiveness of sins: ¹⁵ Who is the image of the invisible God, the firstborn of every creature: ¹⁶ For by him were all things created, that are in heaven, and that are in earth, visible and invisible, whether *they be* thrones, or dominions, or principalities, or powers: all things were created by him, and for him: ¹⁷ And he is before all things, and by him all things consist. ¹⁸ And he is the head of the body, the church: who is the beginning, the firstborn from the dead; that in all *things* he might have the preeminence. ¹⁹ For it pleased *the Father* that in him should all fulness dwell; ²⁰ And, having made peace through the blood of his cross, by him to reconcile all things unto himself; by him, *I say*, whether *they be* things in earth, or things in heaven. ²¹ And you, that were sometime alienated and enemies in *your* mind by wicked works, yet now hath he reconciled

Chapter Eleven
The Provisions of Christ

If you are saved, I want to tell you few things you have in Jesus Christ. If you are not saved, make the decision now to cross the line of faith and place your confidence in the Person, and the atoning work of Jesus Christ on the cross.

- **You Are Related Through A Kingdom Parentage** (*Giving thanks unto the Father*)
- **You Are Regenerated With Kingdom Potential** (*which hath made us meet*)
- **You Are Rewarded A Kingdom Promise** (*partakers of the inheritance of the saints in light*)
- **The Rescued As A Kingdom Purchase** (*in whom we have redeption*)
- **You Are A Resident of A Kingdom Position** (*hath translated us into the kingdom of his dear Son*)
- **You Are Ratified By A Kingdom Payment** (through his blood)
- **The Recipient of A Kingdom Pardon** (even the forgiveness of sin)

The provisions of Christ are immeasurable. When you get in Christ and Christ gets in you, there are eternal blessing that come into your life that will never be taken away. You get kingdom parentage in that God becomes your Father. You get regenerated, born from above, made brand new on the inside. You get a kingdom promise, in that the new heaven and the new earth becomes your new final destination with God throughout eternity. You get eternal rescue from the guilt of sin and the grip of Satan. You become a citizen of heaven and a royal-resident in the kingdom of God. You have the blood of Jesus applied to your life to cover all the sins you've ever committed and ever will commit.

We've already outlined that God is your Father, and therefore, since you have a new Father, you have a new family, a new fortune, and a new future. But think about what else flows from this kingdom parentage that you now enjoy.

Kingdom Position

Ephesians 1:3-7 (KJV)
³ Blessed *be* **the God and Father of our Lord Jesus Christ, who hath blessed us with all spiritual blessings in heavenly** *places* **in Christ: ⁴ According as he hath chosen us in him before the foundation of the world, that we should be holy and without blame before him in love: ⁵ Having predestinated us unto the adoption of children by Jesus Christ to himself, according to the good pleasure of his will, ⁶ To the praise of the glory of his grace, wherein he hath made us accepted in the beloved. ⁷ In whom we**

have redemption through his blood, the forgiveness of sins, according to the riches of his grace;

Scripture tells us that we are blessed in Christ, chosen in Christ, predestinated in Christ, adopted in Christ, accepted in Christ, redeemed in Christ, sealed in Christ, created in Christ, and brought near to God in Christ. We have a kingdom position that was provided by Christ.

Kingdom Potential

Spiritual Vastness (Phil. 4:13))
   – "The Blossoming of Your Life In Christ"
Spiritual Victory (Eph. 6:10-18)
   – "The Battling of Your Life In Christ"
Spiritual Volition (Matt. 5:1-12)
   – The Be-attitudes of Your Life In Christ"
Spiritual Venue (Matt. 5:13-16)
   – "The Brightness of Your Life In Christ"
Spiritual Veracity (Acts 1:8)
   – "The Bold-Witness of Your Life In Christ"
Spiritual Venture (Eph. 3:20-21)
   – "The Bounty of Your Life In Christ"
Spiritual Vision (Matt. 28:18-22)
   – "The Business of Your Life In Christ"

Kingdom people are spiritual giants. Start living up to your potential in Christ. You can do whatever He calls you to do. You can give whatever He asks you to give. You can go wherever He sends you to go. You can witness to whomever He bids you to witness. Christ is your Difference-Maker!

The Distress Principle *God Does Not Send or Allow Distresses To Destroy You, He Sends or Allows Distresses To Develop You*

As you think about "The Distress Principle" above, consider developing and maximizing your potential in these four areas.

- *Your Potential to <u>Continue in Your Situations</u>*
  I. Pet. 1:3-9
- *Your Potential to <u>Conquer Your Sin</u>*
  Rom. 6:1-7
- *Your Potential to <u>Contribute through Your Service</u>*
  I. Cor. 12:1-7; Eph. 4:11-16 &
- *Your Potential to <u>Come Into Your Success</u>*
  Joshua 1:8; Psalm 1:1-3; John 15:1-8**

The Dare Principle *The Size of Your Prayers Reveal The Size of Your Faith*

As you think about "The Dare Principle" above, I want you to consider and commit to doing three things.

- *Ask Great Things of God*: Matt. 6:9-13; 7:7-8; John 15:7;
- *Attempt Great Things for God*: Mal. 1:11; Eph. 2:1-7
- *Expect Great Things from God*: John 15:16; I. John 5:14-15

Chapter Twelve
The Preeminence of Christ

The Apostle Paul was indirectly addressing some heresies that were being taught in Colosse. He did not spend any time identifying and attacking the false teaching, what he did was clearly communicate truth. I'm told that bank tellers are never trained with counterfeit money. They become so familiar with the real, that when the fake is presented they readily identify it. That's how the Holy Ghost wants us to be. He wants us so familiar with the truth of Scripture that whenever we hear or see different we can readily identify it and bring the truth to bear on every conversation and in every situation. In this chapter I want to highlight some truth about Christ. Remember, how you see Christ will determine how you submit to Christ. How you see Christ will determine how you serve Christ. Paul used a term "preeminent," which describes how Jesus is first in rank, in terms of all creation and He is the first to rise victoriously from the dead. I want to look at five ways Paul proclaimed His preeminence.

Christ is Preeminent in Salvation

Colossians 1:14 (KJV)
14 In whom we have redemption through his blood, *even* **the forgiveness of sins:**

No other human being could have died for our salvation. No other human was God enough and man enough at the same time. Jesus had a holy birth. Jesus lived a sinless life, and Jesus died a sacrificial death. Jesus is our High Priest, Jesus is the Mercy-Seat, and Jesus is the Sacrifice that was slain for the sins of the whole world.

Christ is Preeminent in Representation

Colossians 1:15 (KJV)
15 Who is the image of the invisible God, the firstborn of every creature:

That term image (eikon) in the Greek, does not mean resemblance or replica. It means a direct representation. It mean the exact same thing in essence. Jesus Christ on earth was God in the flesh. That's why the Apostle John said, "the Word was made flesh." That term Word is logos, it literally means the mind of God in human form. As confusing as it may be, I must declare unto you, Jesus Christ was and is God.

John 1:1-2 (KJV)
1 In the beginning was the Word, and the Word was with God, and the Word was God.
2 The same was in the beginning with God.

_____
_____
_____

Matthew 1:21-23 (KJV)
²¹ And she shall bring forth a son, and thou shalt call his name JESUS: for he shall save his people from their sins.
²² Now all this was done, that it might be fulfilled which was spoken of the Lord by the prophet, saying,
²³ Behold, a virgin shall be with child, and shall bring forth a son, and they shall call his name Emmanuel, which being interpreted is, God with us.

The Heavenly Father is God for us, the Holy Spirit is God in us, but when Jesus was here on earth He was God with us.

Christ is Preeminent in Creation

Colossians 1:16 (KJV)
¹⁶ For by him were all things created, that are in heaven, and that are in earth, visible and invisible, whether *they be* thrones, or dominions, or principalities, or powers: all things were created by him, and for him:

That phrase "firstborn of every creature" in verse 15 does not mean that He was made before every creature, it means He made every creature. The text says that all things were made by Him and for Him. Notice what John says in the beginning of his gospel.

John 1:3-4 (KJV)
³ All things were made by him; and without him was not any thing made that was made.
⁴ In him was life; and the life was the light of men.

Everything and every person were made by Jesus. He is preeminent in creation. Christ desires our worship, but quite frankly, Christ deserves our worship because He is the Creator of the universe.

Christ is Preeminent in Operation

Colossians 1:18-19 (KJV)
¹⁸ And he is the head of the body, the church: who is the beginning, the firstborn from the dead; that in all *things* he might have the preeminence.
¹⁹ For it pleased *the Father* that in him should all fulness dwell;

Jesus took the sting out of death and robbed the grave of its victory. Jesus is the fullness of the Trinity. Notice what Paul says.
Colossians 2:9-10 (KJV)
⁹ For in him dwelleth all the fulness of the Godhead bodily.
¹⁰ And ye are complete in him, which is the head of all principality and power:

_____
_____
_____
_____

Christ is Preeminent in Reconciliation

Colossians 1:20-22 (KJV)
[20] And, having made peace through the blood of his cross, by him to reconcile all things unto himself; by him, *I say*, whether *they be* things in earth, or things in heaven.
[21] And you, that were sometime alienated and enemies in *your* mind by wicked works, yet now hath he reconciled
[22] In the body of his flesh through death, to present you holy and unblameable and unreproveable in his sight:

Paul gives us a dose of doctrine in three short verses. First he gives us *the doctrine of reconciliation*. To reconcile "katallasso" in the Greek, means remove enmity. It means to be brought back into relationship. It's a picture of the loving choosing to love the unlovable. It is God hugging us back into relationship and fellowship with Him through Jesus Christ.

1 Timothy 2:5 (KJV)
[5] For *there is* one God, and one mediator between God and men, the man Christ Jesus;

He also gives us *the doctrine of alienation*. Man was separated from God. We were at enmity with God. All unsaved, un-regenerated human beings are either passively or actively at war with or opposed to God. But Jesus became God near us and brought us near to God.

Ephesians 2:11-13 (KJV)
¹¹ Wherefore remember, that ye *being* in time past Gentiles in the flesh, who are called Uncircumcision by that which is called the Circumcision in the flesh made by hands;
¹² That at that time ye were without Christ, being aliens from the commonwealth of Israel, and strangers from the covenants of promise, having no hope, and without God in the world:
¹³ But now in Christ Jesus ye who sometimes were far off are made nigh by the blood of Christ.

Finally, he gives us *the doctrine of glorification*. Paul says that He came, He was crucified, and that He conquered death so He could present us holy, unblameable, and unreproavable in His sight. Someone has said that justification means just as if we never sinned. We could look at these words from another perspective. Holy is consecration and sanctification. Blamelessness is justification. And, above reproach is vindication. Wow! Christ has done so much for us and there is still more to come.

The Discovery Principle
The More You Learn About Christ, The More You Love Christ

Devotional Thoughts

_____
_____
_____
_____
_____
_____
_____

Section Four

Principles from the Apostle's Predicament

Colossians 1:24-29 (KJV)
[24] Who now rejoice in my sufferings for you, and fill up that which is behind of the afflictions of Christ in my flesh for his body's sake, which is the church:
[25] Whereof I am made a minister, according to the dispensation of God which is given to me for you, to fulfil the word of God;
[26] *Even* the mystery which hath been hid from ages and from generations, but now is made manifest to his saints:
[27] To whom God would make known what *is* the riches of the glory of this mystery among the Gentiles; which is Christ in you, the hope of glory:
[28] Whom we preach, warning every man, and teaching every man in all wisdom; that we may present every man perfect in Christ Jesus:
[29] Whereunto I also labour, striving according to his working, which worketh in me mightily.

Chapter Thirteen
The Prisoner of Christ

Paul was a preacher, Paul was a practitioner, Paul was a prayer-warrior, but the image that grips me the most is that Paul was a prisoner. He was a prisoner literally. Though he was a literal prisoner, he spoke of himself as the Lord's prisoner.

Ephesians 4:1 (KJV)
1 I therefore, the prisoner of the Lord, beseech you that ye walk worthy of the vocation wherewith ye are called,

Acts 20:17-24 (KJV)
17 And from Miletus he sent to Ephesus, and called the elders of the church. 18 And when they were come to him, he said unto them, Ye know, from the first day that I came into Asia, after what manner I have been with you at all seasons, 19 Serving the Lord with all humility of mind, and with many tears, and temptations, which befell me by the lying in wait of the Jews: 20 *And* how I kept back nothing that was profitable *unto you*, but have shewed you, and have taught you publickly, and from house to house, 21 Testifying both to the Jews, and also to the Greeks, repentance toward God, and faith toward our Lord Jesus Christ. 22 And now, behold, I go bound in the spirit unto Jerusalem, not knowing the things that shall befall me there: 23 Save that the Holy Ghost witnesseth in every city, saying that bonds and afflictions abide me. 24 But none of these things move me, neither count I my life dear unto myself, so that I might finish my course with joy, and the ministry,

which I have received of the Lord Jesus, to testify the gospel of the grace of God.

I think there are some principles to be gleaned from this passage in Colossians that can be applied to our lives today.

Devotional Thoughts

<u>**The Atmosphere of this Prisoner of the Lord**</u>:
→   →   →   →   →

Acts 16:16-34 (KJV)

¹⁶ And it came to pass, as we went to prayer, a certain damsel possessed with a spirit of divination met us, which brought her masters much gain by soothsaying:
¹⁷ The same followed Paul and us, and cried, saying, These men are the servants of the most high God, which shew unto us the way of salvation.
¹⁸ And this did she many days. But Paul, being grieved, turned and said to the spirit, I command thee in the name of Jesus Christ to come out of her. And he came out the same hour.
¹⁹ And when her masters saw that the hope of their gains was gone, <u>they caught Paul and Silas, and drew *them* into the marketplace unto the rulers</u>,
²⁰ And brought them to the magistrates, saying, These men, being Jews, do exceedingly trouble our city,
²¹ And teach customs, which are not lawful for us to receive, neither to observe, being Romans.
²² And the multitude rose up together against them: <u>and the magistrates rent off their clothes, and commanded to beat *them*.</u>
²³ <u>And when they had laid many stripes upon them, they cast *them* into prison, charging the jailor to keep them safely:</u>
²⁴ <u>Who, having received such a charge, thrust them into the inner prison, and made their feet fast in the stocks</u>.
²⁵ And at midnight Paul and Silas prayed, and sang praises unto God: and the prisoners heard them.
²⁶ And suddenly there was a great earthquake, so that the foundations of the prison were shaken: and immediately all the doors were opened, and every one's bands were loosed.
²⁷ And the keeper of the prison awaking out of his

sleep, and seeing the prison doors open, he drew out his sword, and would have killed himself, supposing that the prisoners had been fled.

28 But Paul cried with a loud voice, saying, Do thyself no harm: for we are all here.

29 Then he called for a light, and sprang in, and came trembling, and fell down before Paul and Silas,

30 And brought them out, and said, Sirs, what must I do to be saved?

31 And they said, Believe on the Lord Jesus Christ, and thou shalt be saved, and thy house.

32 And they spake unto him the word of the Lord, and to all that were in his house.

33 And he took them the same hour of the night, and washed *their* stripes; and was baptized, he and all his, straightway.

34 And when he had brought them into his house, he set meat before them, and rejoiced, believing in God with all his house.

These men were bound, they were blasphemed, they were beaten, & they were banded in handcuffs and shackles in a dark-damp dungeon simply for doing the work of Lord. This was the atmosphere. I think I ought to tell you, the world is a dark-damp dungeon to the Christian *(John 3:16-19)*.

Devotional Thoughts

_____
_____
_____
_____
_____
_____

John 15:18-20 (KJV)
[18] If the world hate you, ye know that it hated me before *it hated* you. [19] If ye were of the world, the world would love his own: but because ye are not of the world, but I have chosen you out of the world, therefore the world hateth you. [20]Remember the word that I said unto you, The servant is not greater than his lord. If they have persecuted me, they will also persecute you; if they have kept my saying, they will keep yours also. *(John 16:33)*

John 17:14-18 (KJV)
[14] I have given them thy word; and the world hath hated them, because they are not of the world, even as I am not of the world.
[15] I pray not that thou shouldest take them out of the world, but that thou shouldest keep them from the evil.
[16] They are not of the world, even as I am not of the world.
[17] Sanctify them through thy truth: thy word is truth.
[18] As thou hast sent me into the world, even so have I also sent them into the world.

Devotional Thoughts

_____
_____
_____
_____
_____
_____
_____
_____

Consider with me..........................
The Afflictions of this Prisoner of the Lord:
2 *Corinthians 11:21-28 (KJV)*
²¹ I speak as concerning reproach, as though we had been weak. Howbeit whereinsoever any is bold, (I speak foolishly,) I am bold also.
²² Are they Hebrews? so *am* I. Are they Israelites? so *am* I. Are they the seed of Abraham? so *am* I.
²³ Are they ministers of Christ? (I speak as a fool) I *am* more; in labours more abundant, in stripes above measure, in prisons more frequent, in deaths oft.
²⁴ Of the Jews five times received I forty *stripes* save one.
²⁵ Thrice was I beaten with rods, once was I stoned, thrice I suffered shipwreck, a night and a day I have been in the deep;
²⁶ *In* journeyings often, *in* perils of waters, *in* perils of robbers, *in* perils by *mine own* countrymen, *in* perils by the heathen, *in* perils in the city, *in* perils in the wilderness, *in* perils in the sea, *in* perils among false brethren;
²⁷ In weariness and painfulness, in watchings often, in hunger and thirst, in fastings often, in cold and nakedness.
²⁸ Beside those things that are without, that which cometh upon me daily, the care of all the churches.
The apostle Paul endured many afflictions & I think I ought to warn you, every believer that is committed to the our Savior will have problems out of Satan & his subjects. (*Eph. 6:10-18; 2 Tim. 3:12; Ps. 34:17-19*). Think with me about..................

<u>*The Attitude of this Prisoner of the Lord*</u>:
Philippians 1:1-18 (KJV)
¹ Paul and Timotheus, the servants of Jesus Christ, to all the saints in Christ Jesus which are at Philippi, with the bishops and deacons:
² Grace *be* unto you, and peace, from God our Father, and *from* the Lord Jesus Christ.
³ I thank my God upon every remembrance of you,
⁴ Always in every prayer of mine for you all making request with joy,
⁵ For your fellowship in the gospel from the first day until now;
⁶ Being confident of this very thing, that he which hath begun a good work in you will perform *it* until the day of Jesus Christ:
⁷ Even as it is meet for me to think this of you all, because I have you in my heart; <u>inasmuch as both in my bonds, and in the defence and confirmation of the gospel</u>, ye all are partakers of my grace.
⁸ For God is my record, how greatly I long after you all in the bowels of Jesus Christ.
⁹ And this I pray, that your love may abound yet more and more in knowledge and *in* all judgment;
¹⁰ That ye may approve things that are excellent; that ye may be sincere and without offence till the day of Christ;
¹¹ Being filled with the fruits of righteousness, which are by Jesus Christ, unto the glory and praise of God.
¹² But I would ye should understand, brethren, <u>that the things *which happened* unto me have fallen out rather unto the furtherance of the gospel;</u>
¹³ <u>So that my bonds in Christ are manifest in all the palace, and in all other *places*;</u>
¹⁴ <u>And many of the brethren in the Lord, waxing</u>

<u>confident by my bonds, are much more bold to speak the word without fear.</u>

¹⁵ Some indeed preach Christ even of envy and strife; and some also of good will:

¹⁶ The one preach Christ of contention, not sincerely, supposing to add <u>affliction to my bonds</u>:

¹⁷ But the other of love, knowing that I am set for the defence of the gospel.

¹⁸ What then? notwithstanding, every way, whether in pretence, or in truth, <u>Christ is preached; and I therein do rejoice, yea, and will rejoice</u>.

Paul says he's rejoicing during his prison experience because…
    a. Prison helped be present the gospel to the guards.
    b. Prison helped me prepare leaders.
    c. Prison helped me propel preachers.
    d. Prison helped me proliferate the gospel of Jesus Christ.

Devotional Thoughts

My dears, we have to learn to rejoice in the rough places because God wants to turn those rough places into some redemptive places. James shows us the attitude toward our afflictions and the response toward our rough-places (*James 1:2-4*)

Think with me about..

The Allegiance of this Prisoner of the Lord:
Acts 20:17-20 (KJV)
[17] And from Miletus he sent to Ephesus, and called the elders of the church.
[18] And when they were come to him, he said unto them, Ye know, from the first day that I came into Asia, after what manner I have been with you at all seasons,
[19] Serving the Lord with all humility of mind, and with many tears, and temptations, which befell me by the lying in wait of the Jews:
[20] *And* how I kept back nothing that was profitable *unto you*, but have shewed you, and have taught you publickly, and from house to house,

Acts 20:21-23 (KJV)
[21] Testifying both to the Jews, and also to the Greeks, repentance toward God, and faith toward our Lord Jesus Christ.
[22] And now, behold, I go bound in the spirit unto Jerusalem, not knowing the things that shall befall me there:
[23] Save that the Holy Ghost witnesseth in every city, saying that bonds and afflictions abide me.

Acts 20:24-27 (KJV)
²⁴ But none of these things move me, neither count I my life dear unto myself, so that I might finish my course with joy, and the ministry, which I have received of the Lord Jesus, to testify the gospel of the grace of God.
²⁵ And now, behold, I know that ye all, among whom I have gone preaching the kingdom of God, shall see my face no more.
²⁶ Wherefore I take you to record this day, that I *am* pure from the blood of all *men*.
²⁷ For I have not shunned to declare unto you all the counsel of God.

Paul Essentially Says, I've Been Faithful……
    a. Faithful to the Elders
    b. Faithful to the Eternal-One
    c. Faithful in Expository Preaching & Teaching & I'm not
    d. Fearful of the Evil that will Come Upon Me, but rather
    e. Focused On God's Eternal Purposes for My Life.

That's how the Kingdom Christian is supposed to live----having a clear conscience, because of a constant commitment to the cause of Christ, and having courage in the face of conflict!!!

Philippians 1:19-21 (KJV)
¹⁹ For I know that this shall turn to my salvation through your prayer, and the supply of the Spirit of Jesus Christ, ²⁰ According to my earnest expectation and *my* hope, that in nothing I shall be ashamed, but *that* with all boldness, as always, *so* now also <u>Christ shall be magnified in my body, whether *it be* by life, or by death</u>. ²¹ For to me to live *is* Christ, and to die *is* gain.

Finally my friend, consider with me.....................
<u>The Application of the prisoner of the Lord</u>: (24-29)
- A Prisoner of *Appreciation* (who now rejoice)
- A Prisoner of *Afflictions* (my suffering)
- A Prisoner to *Adherents* (for his body's sake..)
- A Prisoner of *Assignment* (made a minister)
- A Prisoner of *the Almighty* (dispensation of God)
- A Prisoner of *His Agenda* (fulfill the word of God)
- A Prisoner of *His Atonement* (Christ in you)
- A Prisoner of the *Announcement* (preach/warning)
- A Prisoner of *Assistance* (teaching)
- A Prisoner of *Alignment* (present every man)
- A Prisoner of *Advancement* (perfect in Christ Jesus)
- A Prisoner of the *Altar* (whereunto I also labor)

I believe that the things listed represent the things we ought to be committed to, the things that we ought to be voluntarily bound to. Most of them we've discussed so I'm only going to pull some principles from a few.

When God Wants A Man

When God wants to drill a man,
And thrill a man,
And skill a man
When God wants to mold a man
To play the noblest part;

When He yearns with all His heart
To create so great and bold a man
That all the world shall be amazed,
Watch His methods, watch His ways!

How He ruthlessly perfects
Whom He royally elects!
How He hammers him and hurts him,
And with mighty blows converts him

Into trial shapes of clay which
Only God understands;
While his tortured heart is crying
And he lifts beseeching hands!

How He bends but never breaks
When his good He undertakes;
How He uses whom He chooses,
And with every purpose fuses him;
By every act induces him
To try His splendor out-
God knows what He's all about.

The poet is pointing out that God breaks us to build us, God crushes us to construct us, God permits our misery, to perfect our ministries!!!!

A Prisoner of Appreciation (who now rejoice): that term rejoice in the Greek is chairo, it means to be cheerful, to be glad, and to be calmly happy. The Christian ought to be held captive by appreciation to the Lord regardless of our situations or circumstances. Notice what Paul says in Phil. 4:4-7

- *Rejoice with your Requests*
  4 Rejoice in the Lord alway: and again I say, Rejoice. 5 Let your moderation be known unto all men. The Lord is at hand. 6 Be careful for nothing; but in every thing by prayer and supplication with thanksgiving let your requests be made known unto God. 7 And the peace of God, which passeth all understanding, shall keep your hearts and minds through Christ Jesus.

- *Rejoice Regularly*
  1 Thessalonians 5:16-18 (KJV)
  16 Rejoice evermore. 17 Pray without ceasing. 18 In every thing give thanks: for this is the will of God in Christ Jesus concerning you.

Peter says to us.....
- **Rejoice when it gets Rough:**
  1 Peter 1:3-9 (KJV)

3 Blessed be the God and Father of our Lord Jesus Christ, which according to his abundant mercy hath begotten us again unto a lively hope by the resurrection of Jesus Christ from the dead, 4 To an inheritance incorruptible, and undefiled, and that fadeth not away, reserved in heaven for you, 5 Who are kept by the power of God through faith unto salvation ready to be revealed in the last time. 6 Wherein ye greatly rejoice, though now for a season, if need be, ye are in heaviness through manifold temptations: 7 That the trial of your faith, being much more precious than of gold that perisheth, though it be tried with fire, might be found unto praise and honour and glory at the appearing of Jesus Christ: 8 Whom having not seen, ye love; in whom, though now ye see him not, yet believing, ye rejoice with joy unspeakable and full of glory: 9 Receiving the end of your faith, even the salvation of your souls.

_____

_____

_____

A Prisoner of Afflictions

(in my sufferings for you): that term sufferings in Greek is pathema, it means undergoing hardships and/or pain. What we gather from the life and leadership of the Apostle Paul is that the surrendered saint will be subject to attacks, abhorrence, and afflictions.

Attacks from Satan (Eph. 6:10-18; I. Pet. 5:6-11),

Abhorrence from Sinners (2 Tim. 3:12), and
Afflictions from Situations (Ps. 34:17-19).

Notice what Paul tells Timothy & us in....
2 Timothy 3:12 (KJV)
12 Yea, and all that will live godly in Christ Jesus shall suffer persecution.

My dears we suffer because Christ suffered and we are to suffer like Christ suffered. Christ suffered with class, with compassion, with commitment, and with confidence.

Notice what Peter says in.....
Acceptable in our Suffering
1 Peter 2:19-25 (KJV)
19 For this is thankworthy, if a man for conscience toward God endure grief, suffering wrongfully.
20 For what glory is it, if, when ye be buffeted for your faults, ye shall take it patiently? but if, when ye do well, and suffer for it, ye take it patiently, this is acceptable with God.
21 For even hereunto were ye called: because Christ also suffered for us, leaving us an example, that ye should follow his steps:
22 Who did no sin, neither was guile found in his mouth:
23 Who, when he was reviled, reviled not again; when he suffered, he threatened not; but committed himself to him that judgeth righteously:
24 Who his own self bare our sins in his own body on the tree, that we, being dead to sins, should live unto righteousness: by whose stripes ye were healed.

25 For ye were as sheep going astray; but are now returned unto the Shepherd and Bishop of your souls.

A Prisoner to Adherents

(for you; his body's sake; which is the church): That term church is ekklesia in the Greek, it means called-out ones. We are called out of darkness into light, called out of the world, into His Word, called out of sin & selfishness into sanctification and service. The child of God must be given to the Church of God. The growing Christian must be given to helping other Christians grow. The Christian that has come through some storms, must be committed to comforting other Christians who are going through the storm. Notice what the apostle Paul says in   Galatians 1:6-10.
Devotional Thoughts

Galatians 6:1-10 (KJV) 1 Brethren, if a man be overtaken in a fault, ye which are spiritual, restore such an one in the spirit of meekness; considering thyself, lest thou also be tempted. 2 Bear ye one another's burdens, and so fulfil the law of Christ. 3 For if a man think himself to be something, when he is nothing, he deceiveth himself. 4 But let every man prove his own work, and then shall he have rejoicing in himself alone, and not in another. 5 For every man shall bear his own burden. 6 Let him that is taught in the word communicate unto him that teacheth in all good things. 7 Be not deceived; God is not mocked: for whatsoever a man soweth, that shall he also reap. 8 For he that soweth to his flesh shall of the flesh reap corruption; but he that soweth to the Spirit shall of the Spirit reap life everlasting. 9 And let us not be weary in well doing: for in due season we shall reap, if we faint not. 10 As we have therefore opportunity, let us do good unto all men, especially unto them who are of the household of faith.

Paul says that we ought to
RESTORE fallen saints,
RELIEVE burdened saints,
RESOURCE the pastor who teaches you the Word, &
RESPOND to every need that we can, especially the needs of those who are of the household of faith.

Notice how he tells the church at Ephesus that every member of the body of Christ is important to the kingdom of God.

REPRODUCE in the Kingdom

Ephesians 4:11-16 (KJV)
11 And he gave some, apostles; and some, prophets; and some, evangelists; and some, pastors and teachers; 12 For the perfecting of the saints, for the work of the ministry, for the edifying of the body of Christ: 13 Till we all come in the unity of the faith, and of the knowledge of the Son of God, unto a perfect man, unto the measure of the stature of the fulness of Christ: 14 That we henceforth be no more children, tossed to and fro, and carried about with every wind of doctrine, by the sleight of men, and cunning craftiness, whereby they lie in wait to deceive; 15 But speaking the truth in love, may grow up into him in all things, which is the head, even Christ: 16 From whom the whole body fitly joined together and compacted by that which every joint supplieth, according to the effectual working in the measure of every part, maketh increase of the body unto the edifying of itself in love.

A Prisoner of Assignment *(whereof I am made a minister)*
That term made in the Greek is ginomai, it means to cause to be, to produce, and to generate. That term minister in the Greek is diakonos, it means to serve, it carries the connotation of one who waits tables, one who runs errands, & one who lives for the pleasure of another. Jesus essentially said about Himself....

I Came To Serve:

Mark 10:45; John 6:37-38 (KJV)
37 All that the Father giveth me shall come to me; and him that cometh to me I will in no wise cast out. 38 For I came down from heaven, not to do mine own will, but the will of him that sent me.

John 6:37-38 (KJV)
37 All that the Father giveth me shall come to me; and him that cometh to me I will in no wise cast out.
38 For I came down from heaven, not to do mine own will, but the will of him that sent me.

John 9:1-4 (KJV)
1 And as Jesus passed by, he saw a man which was blind from his birth. 2 And his disciples asked him, saying, Master, who did sin, this man, or his parents, that he was born blind? 3 Jesus answered, Neither hath this man sinned, nor his parents: but that the works of God should be made manifest in him. 4 I must work the works of him that sent me, while it is day: the night cometh, when no man can work.

Devotional Thoughts

_____
_____
_____
_____
_____
_____
_____
_____
_____
_____

I Commissioned You To Serve:

John 17:17-21 (KJV)
17 Sanctify them through thy truth: thy word is truth. 18 As thou hast sent me into the world, even so have I also sent them into the world. 19 And for their sakes I sanctify myself, that they also might be sanctified through the truth. 20 Neither pray I for these alone, but for them also which shall believe on me through their word; 21 That they all may be one; as thou, Father, art in me, and I in thee, that they also may be one in us: that the world may believe that thou hast sent me.

John 20:21 (KJV)
21 Then said Jesus to them again, Peace be unto you: as my Father hath sent me, even so send I you.

I Crafted You To Serve

Ephesians 2:8-10 (KJV) (I. Pet.4:10)
8 For by grace are ye saved through faith; and that not of yourselves: it is the gift of God:9 Not of works, lest any man should boast. 10 For we are his workmanship, created in Christ Jesus unto good works, which God hath before ordained that we should walk in them.

Every believer is made for ministry, we are saved for service, we are redeemed for reproduction, we are graciously converted to carry-out the Great Commission, and we have been revolutionized to be become revolutionaries. Let's go be change-agents for Jesus Christ! Stay Encouraged!!!!

About The Author

Pastor Reginald D. Taylor acknowledged the call to preach July 13, 1993 and was licensed and ordained to preach the Gospel of Jesus Christ under the leadership of Dr. Frank E. Ray Sr. September 12, 1993. Pastor Taylor holds an A. S. degree in General Studies from Shelby State Community College, a B. S. in Biblical Studies from Crichton College of Memphis, & a Master of Christian Studies from Union University. Pastor Taylor is certified in Urban Youth Evangelism and Urban Youth Discipleship through Youth For Christ International. He is certified in Essentials of Expository Preaching through the Stephen Olford Institute of Expository Preaching. -Reginald D. Taylor has traveled extensively preaching and teaching the Word of God. He serves the body of Christ as a leadership-coach, community-developer, author, conference-speaker, Bible Instructor and Church Planter. Pastor Taylor is an Adjunct Instructor in The School of Theology & Missions @ The Stephen Olford Center at Union University in Memphis, TN. He has been referred to as "The Walking Bible" due to his massive memorization and recall of Scripture.

-He served as Minister of Outreach at New Salem M. B. Church and as Assistant Pastor/Project Manager at Cummings Street M. B. Church both of Memphis.

-Reginald D. Taylor lives in Horn Lake MS. with his wife Dr. Tarra Renee Taylor, they have one son Reginald D. Taylor II. He is available for teaching, preaching, leadership-training, counseling, weddings and funerals. Contact him at **(901) 258-2876 or reginaldtaylorministries@gmail.com**

©The Prepared Life, Reginald D. Taylor 2014

END NOTES

[i] I heard Pastor Robert Smith tell this story in a sermon titled, "Be Careful Who You Hang With'" in 2005.

[ii] Osbeck, Kenneth W. Amazing Grace: 366 Hymn Stories for Personal Devotions. Grand Rapids MI. Kregal Publications 1990

[iii] **Colossians 3:16-17 (KJV)**
16 Let the word of Christ dwell in you richly in all wisdom; teaching and admonishing one another in psalms and hymns and spiritual songs, singing with grace in your hearts to the Lord.
17 And whatsoever ye do in word or deed, *do* all in the name of the Lord Jesus, giving thanks to God and the Father by him.

[iv] **Romans 1:11 (KJV)**
11 For I long to see you, that I may impart unto you some spiritual gift, to the end ye may be established;

[v] **1 Corinthians 1:4-9 (KJV)**
4 I thank my God always on your behalf, for the grace of God which is given you by Jesus Christ;
5 That in every thing ye are enriched by him, in all utterance, and *in* all knowledge;
6 Even as the testimony of Christ was confirmed in you:
7 So that ye come behind in no gift; waiting for the coming of our Lord Jesus Christ:
8 Who shall also confirm you unto the end, *that ye may be* blameless in the day of our Lord Jesus Christ.
9 God *is* faithful, by whom ye were called unto the fellowship of his Son Jesus Christ our Lord.

[vi] **Galatians 5:1 (KJV)**
1 Stand fast therefore in the liberty wherewith Christ hath made us free, and be not entangled again with the yoke of bondage.

[vii] **Ephesians 3:14-19 (KJV)**
14 For this cause I bow my knees unto the Father of our Lord Jesus Christ,
15 Of whom the whole family in heaven and earth is named,
16 That he would grant you, according to the riches of his glory, to be strengthened with might by his Spirit in the inner man;
17 That Christ may dwell in your hearts by faith; that ye, being rooted and grounded in love,
18 May be able to comprehend with all saints what *is* the breadth, and length, and depth, and height;
19 And to know the love of Christ, which passeth knowledge, that ye might be filled with all the fulness of God.

[viii]**Philippians 1:9-11 (KJV)**
9 And this I pray, that your love may abound yet more and more in knowledge and *in* all judgment;
10 That ye may approve things that are excellent; that ye may be sincere and without offence till the day of Christ;
11 Being filled with the fruits of righteousness, which are by Jesus Christ, unto the glory and praise of God.

[ix] **Romans 12:3-8 (KJV)**
3 For I say, through the grace given unto me, to every man that is among you, not to think *of himself* more highly than he ought to think; but to think soberly, according as God hath dealt to every man the measure of faith.
4 For as we have many members in one body, and all members have not the same office:
5 So we, *being* many, are one body in Christ, and every one members one of another.
6 Having then gifts differing according to the grace that is given to us, whether prophecy, *let us prophesy* according to the proportion of faith;
7 Or ministry, *let us wait* on *our* ministering: or he that teacheth, on teaching;
8 Or he that exhorteth, on exhortation: he that giveth, *let him do it* with simplicity; he that ruleth, with diligence; he that sheweth mercy, with cheerfulness.

[x] **Ephesians 4:11-16 (KJV)**
11 And he gave some, apostles; and some, prophets; and some, evangelists; and some, pastors and teachers;
12 For the perfecting of the saints, for the work of the ministry, for the edifying of the body of Christ:
13 Till we all come in the unity of the faith, and of the knowledge of the Son of God, unto a perfect man, unto the measure of the stature of the fulness of Christ:
14 That we *henceforth* be no more children, tossed to and fro, and carried about with every wind of doctrine, by the sleight of men, *and* cunning craftiness, whereby they lie in wait to deceive;
15 But speaking the truth in love, may grow up into him in all things, which is the head, *even* Christ:
16 From whom the whole body fitly joined together and compacted by that which every joint supplieth, according to the effectual working in the measure of every part, maketh increase of the body unto the edifying of itself in love.

[xi] **1 Corinthians 12:4-7 (KJV)**
4 Now there are diversities of gifts, but the same Spirit.
5 And there are differences of administrations, but the same Lord.
6 And there are diversities of operations, but it is the same God which worketh all in all.
7 But the manifestation of the Spirit is given to every man to profit withal.

[xii] **Romans 12:1-2 (KJV)**
1 I beseech you therefore, brethren, by the mercies of God, that ye present your bodies a living sacrifice, holy, acceptable unto God, *which is* your reasonable service.
2 And be not conformed to this world: but be ye transformed by the renewing of your mind, that ye may prove what *is* that good, and acceptable, and perfect, will of God.

[xiii] **Hebrews 4:14-16 (KJV)**
14 Seeing then that we have a great high priest, that is passed into the heavens, Jesus the Son of God, let us hold fast *our* profession.
15 For we have not an high priest which cannot be touched with the feeling of our infirmities; but was in all points tempted like as *we are, yet* without sin.
16 Let us therefore come boldly unto the throne of grace, that we may obtain mercy, and find grace to help in time of need.

[xiv] **Hebrews 12:1-2 (KJV)**
1 Wherefore seeing we also are compassed about with so great a cloud of witnesses, let us lay aside every weight, and the sin which doth so easily beset *us*, and let us run with patience the race that is set before us,
2 Looking unto Jesus the author and finisher of *our* faith; who for the joy that was set before him endured the cross, despising the shame, and is set down at the right hand of the throne of God.

xv John 1:10-13 (KJV)
10 He was in the world, and the world was made by him, and the world knew him not.
11 He came unto his own, and his own received him not.
12 But as many as received him, to them gave he power to become the sons of God, *even* to them that believe on his name:
13 Which were born, not of blood, nor of the will of the flesh, nor of the will of man, but of God.

xvi Maxwell, John C. The 17 Indisputable Laws of Teamwork. Nelson Books 2001

xvii I heard John Maxwell say that phrase in 2007 on a CD from the Maximum Impact Club and it has gripped, guided, and galvanized me ever since. John said, Growth is not an automatic process. He also said, "Motivation will get you going but discipline keeps you growing."

xviii Chapell, Bryan. Christ-Centered Preaching. Baker Academic 2005

Principles of Growth

1. The Devotion Principle: *Growth Is Not An Automatic Process* (II. Timothy 2:15; I. Cor. 9:24-27
2. The Distance Principle: *Growth Is The Great Separator Between Those Who Succeed & Those Who Do Not* (John 15:1-11, 16)
3. The Durability Principle: *Growth Takes Time & Only Time Can Teach You Some Things* (Prov. 3:1-10; Is. 40:31; Ps. 27:13-14)
4. The Demand Principle: *The More We Grow The More We Know We Need To Grow* (I. John 1:7; Ps. 119:17-18, 105)
5. The Deal Principle: *Growth Equals Change* (James 1:21-25; Joshua 3:5; Ps. 119:59-60
6. The Destiny Principle: *Growth Inside Fuels Growth Outside* (Matt. 5:1-16; 6:31-33; 7:24-27)
7. The Deception Principle: *If What You Did Before Still Looks Big To You Then You Are Not Growing* (Joshua 1:1-8)

8. The Dogmatic Principle: *You Must Take Responsibility For Your Own Growth* (I. Pet. 2:2; Ps. 119:9-16; Ps. 1:1-3)
9. The Distinguish Principle: *You Must Determine The Areas In Your Life That Need Growth* (II. Tim. 3:16-17; II. Pet. 1:3-8; Eph. 6:10-18)
10. The Dynamic Principle: *Growth Is Inspired By Growing Individuals & Growing Institutions* (Prov. 27:17; I. Cor. 15:33; Eph. 4:11-16)
11. The Development Principle: *Your Progress Comes Only Through The Process* (I. Chr. 16:11; Prov. 8:34-35; Luke 9:23; I. Cor. 15:58)

Many of these principles I was introduced to through reading John Maxwell's books or listening to him speaking. I've read twenty-five of his books and I listen to him all the time. So, I've simply taken some of the principles I learned from John and repackaged them with alliteration and Scripture. I'm not trying to plagiarize nor be original, I'm trying to offer some life-changing principles that I've incorporated in my own life and am better for it.

Made in the USA
Monee, IL
23 November 2019